⊗ *The Atonement*

PROBLEMS IN THEOLOGY

In the study of Christian theology, there have been, over the centuries, a number of problems for which no adequate explanation has yet been given, or at least, none given which commands substantial agreement among those whose task it is to explain the faith. Some of these issues are central to the understanding of Christianity – the nature of Christ's presence in the Eucharist, for example, or the need for, and the achievement of, redemption. Books in this series will look at crucial topics of this kind. Written by experts, each volume will both trace the history of attempts to answer a particular problem in theology, and then propose a new understanding of the doctrine under debate. Though based upon the latest scholarship, the books are intended for the serious enquirer as much as for the professional theologian.

Already published:

The Atonement
MICHAEL WINTER

The Eucharist
RAYMOND MOLONEY SJ

MICHAEL WINTER

PROBLEMS IN THEOLOGY

The Atonement

A Michael Glazier Book
 THE LITURGICAL PRESS
Collegeville, Minnesota

Published in the UK by Geoffrey Chapman, a Cassell imprint, London
Published in the United States of America and in Canada by
The Liturgical Press, Collegeville, Minnesota

Library of Congress Cataloging-in-Publication Data
Winter, Michael M.
    The Atonement / Michael Winter.
      p.   cm. – (Problems in theology)
    'A Michael Glazier book.'
    Includes bibliographical references and index.
    ISBN 0–8146–5852–0
    1. Atonement.   I. Title.   II. Series.
BT265.2.W57   1994
234'.5–dc20   94–32617
                                                          CIP

Biblical quotations are taken from the Revised Standard Version,
© Copyright 1973 by Division of Christian Education of the National
Council of the Churches of Christ in the United States of America.

Typeset by York House Typographic Ltd, London
Printed and bound in Great Britain by
Biddles Ltd, Guildford and King's Lynn

⊠ *Contents*

⊠ *Introduction*

In recent years there has been a reasonably prolific output of books on the atonement. Yet their very number and mutual disagreements indicate that the main problems are still unresolved, and consequently an entirely new approach is called for.

On the one hand there is an almost universal consensus that explanations along the lines of compensation (or satisfaction), ultimately traceable to St Anselm, are now untenable. This applies to his own straightforward legalistic theory of quasi-compensation to God for the affront done to his honour by sin, and also to theories of penal substitution in which Christ is deemed to have taken on himself the punishment for the sins of the human race. Due credit has been accorded to Anselm for his theory, because he did indeed present a rational solution to the problem. However the reasons which were convincing to him and his contemporaries no longer command assent among religious thinkers today, for reasons which I will show later.

In what one might call the post-Anselmian vacuum there has been an unusual dichotomy. It has been filled by a variety of hypotheses which range from those who present nothing more than a preacher's paradox, and at the other extreme there are writers who disclaim a rational solution at all. By preacher's paradox I mean all those literary devices which are so effective in a homily, and which draw attention to the contrasts inherent in the crucifixion, namely that it was the giver of life who died, the omnipotent one who was crushed by weakness, or the only sinless member of the human race who somehow extinguished the sins of everyone else. Such literary or oratorical devices may be effective in a sermon where the lack of time prevents any more detailed explanation of what actually happened. But as the culmination of a theological investigation they can hardly claim to have provided a solution to the problems. The other school maintains in practice (or by implication) either that the process is ultimately mysterious, or that reverence requires a respectful silence in the presence of so awe-inspiring a transaction.

The result is that the modern reader still lacks a cogent account of how exactly the human race was reconciled to God the Father, and it is my modest intention to fill this gap and offer what I consider to be an intellectually satisfying solution which is compatible with the Scriptures and Tradition, as well as being acceptable to the reasonable expectations of the modern mind.

Because the subject matter of the atonement is closely related to several other branches of theology, one must adopt a self-denying ordinance, so as to exclude those matters which are not absolutely central to the theme, otherwise the book would be of unmanageable length. For example there are obvious links with the doctrines of grace, and the whole area of conversion, moral choices and faith. The sacraments too are closely linked as the means of bestowing on individuals the benefits of the atonement. It goes without saying that the whole field is linked with, and presupposes, the theology of the incarnation. In order to keep the text within reasonable bounds I will presuppose a knowledge of those matters, and in Chapter 1 I will indicate the boundaries within which I will conduct this exploration. In other words I will mention those matters which I am leaving to one side, in order to keep this book within manageable size.

MICHAEL M. WINTER

1

⊠ *Preliminary considerations*

Several years ago I was asked by an agnostic 'Why did Jesus have to die on the cross?' Years of reading and reflection have convinced me that the answer to that basic question is simply that it was not necessary for Jesus to have suffered the crucifixion. (To set everyone's mind at rest I would like to mention that St Thomas Aquinas gave the same answer to what was basically the same question.[1])

Having stated that the crucifixion of Jesus was not strictly necessary, I realize that I have planted in the reader's mind a problem of seemingly intractable difficulty. How does one reconcile that claim with the Christian tradition that the passion and death of Christ were central to the whole process of salvation? No simple answer can be given at this stage, but the solution of that problem is precisely why I decided to write this book. In the pages which follow I hope to give a satisfactory account of how the crucifixion was literally a cause of the atonement, and yet in the last analysis the cruel death was not absolutely necessary. Superficially it appears that I am presenting the reader with a contradiction in terms, yet if the reader will bear with me patiently I am confident that I can clarify the apparent contradiction.

Before pursuing these preliminary considerations further, I feel that it is right to state my debt to the work of Raymund Schwager. His book on the atonement, *Brauchen wir einen Sündenbock?*,[2] is of fundamental importance. I will refer to it at various points in the following chapters. His ideas represent a decisive shift in the whole approach to the questions of sin and redemption. Other writers who have written on this field are almost too numerous to name. I will summarize their views in the course of this book, but I will not devote a great deal of space to explaining what has been elucidated already, and where a fair measure of consensus has been achieved.

In the remainder of this chapter I will delineate the area of enquiry, and mark off those fields of study which are related to the atonement, but which are dealt with satisfactorily in countless standard works, and which will need no more than a cursory mention in this book.

To begin with, what exactly is meant by the atonement? Briefly it can be described as the restoration of a reciprocal relationship of love between God the Father and the human race. In Chapter 5 I will elaborate this concept more fully, but for the present the brief description just enunciated will suffice. The individuals who enjoy this privileged relationship are recast interiorly so that they can respond to this love and lead lives which are inspired by the love of God and neighbour. Behind that simple statement lies the whole theology of grace, which has been elaborated in countless books, where a large measure of agreement exists between the experts, and which I will therefore leave to one side, knowing that the reader can find it easily elsewhere.

The life of grace does not stay confined within the soul of the believer. It gives him or her[3] the moral strength and energy to overcome the effects of other people's wickedness which militate against his own integrity, rights, and ability to lead the kind of life which God expects of truly human beings. This derivative aspect of the life of grace is expressed with incomparable beauty and force in the well-known prayer, the Benedictus, in whose central section we read the words:

> He swore to Abraham our father to grant us,
> that free from fear, and saved from the hands of our foes,
> we might serve him in holiness and justice.
>
> (Luke 1:73–75)

This is the starting point of Liberation Theology, which is now a well-developed field in its own right, and which lies outside the limits of the present investigation. I merely refer my readers to the many admirable books of Gustavo Gutiérrez, Leonardo Boff, Paulo Freire, Juan Luis Segundo and others. What they have written is germane to the theme of this enquiry, but it would be superfluous to repeat what is readily available elsewhere. There is however just one writer whom I would like to mention in connection with the principle that grace is not to be confined within the soul of the individual, and that is Jürgen Moltmann. In his *Theology of Hope* he presented the crucial insight that theology should not be concerned simply with interpreting the past (no matter how momentous the events may have been) but it must also concern itself with transforming the present world.[4] Readers will doubtless note the resemblance to Marx's famous dictum that philosophers had endeavoured to understand the world, but the important point was to change it. It should not cause us any worry that Moltmann was influenced by Marx. It is not the first time that Christian theology has employed the insights and intellectual categories of non-believing philosophers.

The third effect of the life of grace or salvation (whichever one likes to call it) is the believer's reaction to a situation where he cannot overcome the wickedness which is coming from outside. He may be the helpless victim of a situation of economic exploitation, or perhaps the persecution of the Church. What help does grace give him in that kind of situation? It enables him to live with an attitude of optimistic determination that no amount of pressure will deter him from pursuing the Christian ideals in his own life, and in his political activities striving for a just society in which to live. The words 'optimistic determination' are the most satisfactory translation that I can think of for the virtue which the New Testament calls *hupomonē* and which is frequently rendered as 'patient endurance'. That translation does not really do justice to the positive overtones of the Greek *hupomonē*, particularly in view of the passive overtones of the English word 'patience'. This is the virtue which sustained the martyrs in times of persecution. They could not convert their persecutors to Christianity, but they held fast to their convictions in the face of every conceivable adversity and suffering, even to the point of death. It is a very positive and creative effect of the life of grace, even when all exterior circumstances militate against the visible success of the Christian message. It is the same virtue which now gives strength to civil rights activists and trade union militants in places like Latin America where Christians are in the vanguard of movements for social justice and where the chances of success seem remote. This aspect of the life of grace has been studied elsewhere;[5] so I will not pursue the matter further.

Another related topic in the area of grace is that of original sin. This too has been studied by countless theologians whose conclusions can be found in all the standard textbooks. I mention it here, merely to point out that were it not for the widespread occurrence of evil, which has its ultimate source in original sin, there would be no need for a redeemer and for the work of atonement. The precise nature of original sin and its connection with mankind's enduring wickedness has been greatly disputed. It need not delay us in this study. I wish simply to draw the reader's attention to two points, namely the plain fact of evil, and the impossibility of accounting for it in purely human terms such as emotional deprivation in infancy. An assessment of the reality and power of evil will depend on an individual's outlook on life. Some people are extremely naïve about the niceness of the world in which we live. However I am convinced that no serious-minded person with any experience of life can escape the realization of just how dreadful is the moral conduct of most of us in the human race.

The persistence of warfare as a means of settling international disputes is itself incontrovertible evidence of our badness. When one begins to examine other areas of evil the list is seemingly unlimited. About twenty years ago it was calculated that the whole human race could have been given adequate housing, education, clean drinking water, and medical care at a fraction of the sum which was then disbursed annually for armaments. A few years ago certain nations swiftly acquired great wealth thanks to their oil revenues. The money was invested via the World Bank in the developing countries. Why was it invested (thereby creating the Debt Problem on account of interest repayments) instead of being given to the poor countries, like Marshall Aid at the end of the Second World War? The list of iniquities could be prolonged indefinitely, but I would like to quote one more piece of evidence, namely the basic facts researched for the World Assembly of Christian Churches which met in Seoul in 1990:

Every minute the nations of the world spend 1.8 millions of US dollars on military armaments. Every hour 1500 children die of hunger related causes. Every day a species becomes extinct. Every week during the 1980's more people were detained, tortured, assassinated, made refugees, or in other ways violated by acts of repressive regimes than at any other time in history except World War II. Every month the world's economic system adds over 7.5 billions of US dollars to the catastrophically unbearable debt burden of more than 1500 billion dollars now resting on the shoulders of the Third World peoples. Every year an area of tropical forest three quarters the size of Korea is destroyed and lost.[6]

At the root of all these economic or military decisions we find moral choices, such as the choice to make a profit for the owners of the petrodollars, or to make a gift to the poorer nations. I wish to emphasize that they are moral choices, to which we can, and must, respond with free rational decisions. They are not simply the aberrations caused by economic forces or psychological factors in infancy. Admittedly the conduct of many so-called deviant individuals can be understood, and perhaps rectified by psychological investigation and treatment. But I am convinced that the constant pattern of behaviour of the vast majority of the human race, involving so much greed, aggression, violence, and lies, cannot be accounted for in terms of simple psychological cause and effect. It is too widespread and too constant among peoples of all cultures and every epoch. A much deeper and more powerful cause must be found. As a believing Christian I have no difficulty in tracing it to original sin, which denotes a propensity to evil in all of us, which can be put right only by inner strength from God.

This is why the human race needs religion, and at the heart of it lies the struggle to overcome evil, which is the immediate context for the work of the atonement.

Unfortunately religion is not always seen in this light. Many people retain an impression of primitive rites practised in the remote past to ensure the fertility of crops and herds or to ward off evil influences. Superficially it might appear that this kind of attitude underpinned medieval religion, which could have been influential in people's lives largely on account of their ignorance of the scientific processes which controlled disease, climate, fertility and other vital necessities for life. The same line of thought would seek to explain the demise of religion in the modern world simply because scientific methods for farming, medicine and the rest have replaced the superstitious practices of primitive religion. A thoughtful reading of the New Testament ought to convince an open-minded person that this is not the case. The religion which is contained in its pages had already leap-frogged the system of nature religion (for want of a better word). The New Testament contains nothing about warding off the evil eye, nor about rain-making, nor about any of the other processes with which primitive pagan religions were so anxiously preoccupied. It is concerned almost exclusively with moral choices and personal relationships. Paradoxically the development of modern science has emphasized the need for this kind of authentic religion, since the worst evils of the human race are not solved by chemical fertilizers but depend upon free choices. Science has proved totally incapable of providing a remedy for violence, greed, and exploitative relationships. These evils can be cured only by the moral resources of individuals, which is the arena of temptation, sin, redemption, and virtue. If religion has been marginalized in the latter part of the twentieth century, it has only itself to blame for failing to apply its influence and moral resources to the real areas of human suffering and evil. To cite just one example, instead of devoting so much passion to the debate about the ordination of women, the Churches would have done better had they devoted their energies to campaigning for the emancipation of women in most societies of the world. In the majority of cultures they are still condemned to a subservient position in their societies. Fortunately the omissions are being made good in some parts of the world, particularly in those areas where Liberation Theology flourishes, and where its derivative institutions like basic communities are thriving. I will not pursue this theme further, but it is useful for the reader to keep it in mind, since it provides part of the context within which I will present the theology of the atonement, and it should also remind us of its relevance.

At this point it may be useful to make clear my own preference for a couple of technical terms. For various reasons I prefer to use the word 'atonement' rather than 'redemption'. It carries no overtones of legalism, and is intensely positive in its depicting the reconciliation effected by Christ. One can only marvel at the insight of some unknown genius far back in the history of English Christianity who coined the word to denote the restoration of unity between God and the human race who were thenceforth at one. In this field of theology the other well-known word about which I am unhappy is 'salvation'. It has been overexposed and its meaning has been debased by trivialization in poor-quality hymns and prayers which have not conveyed its authentic meaning. 'Are you saved, brother?' has become a comic cliché in our language. Countless hymns use the word with thoughtless hyperbole, apparently to jolt the lukewarm back into fervour by stressing their supposed sinfulness. Doubtless it was all motivated by sincere convictions, but it has contributed to making the very notion of salvation almost meaningless. In the light of modern English usage the word 'liberation' is a more exact translation of the Hebrew and Greek words which were formerly rendered as 'salvation'. The same applies to 'saviour' and 'saving', which are best translated as 'liberator' and 'liberating'. I cannot promise total consistency in the pages which follow (particularly where I am quoting from other authors), but I feel that the reader would want to know why the traditional words like 'salvation' and 'redemption' do not feature very prominently in the pages of this book.

For some people the theology of atonement presents no real problem at all. They are the holders of a mythological view of religion. If the whole process of religion is basically a projection of subconscious needs, like the quest for a father figure, then it scarcely matters what myth is employed to express the sentiments. By the same token it hardly matters if one mythological formulation has to be abandoned in favour of another. If modern sensibilities find the crucifixion too distasteful, then some other imagery can surely be found which will help the modern mind to find meaning and security in a confusing world. The answer to this kind of difficulty will not be found in assessing the relative values of different mythological presentations of perennial dramas but in the deeper issue of the reality or not of persons and events with which religion has traditionally been concerned. This book is being written on a different wavelength altogether. I am presupposing a traditional belief in God and in the reality of his interaction with his creatures. Ultimately he is mysterious because he is infinite. In spite of considerable intellectual difficulties, of which I am well aware, it is possible to have some reliable knowledge of this mysterious God and his activities. Although our appreciation of him will sometimes be expressed in poetic or mythological imagery, the understanding of his ways is not confined to those literary forms.

For another category of people the Christian doctrine of liberation (or salvation) centred upon the crucifixion is an insuperable barrier to belief in the kind of God who would require such a process to take place in his honour. This group comprises a large number of atheists and former believers who deserve to be taken very seriously because the central position accorded to the passion and death of Jesus constitutes an obstacle to an otherwise sympathetic attitude to religion and the values which Christianity embodies. As this attitude towards religion, and particularly towards the theology of atonement, is widespread in our post-Christian society I will quote a number of such writers verbatim, since their own words express authentically the difficulties inherent in this sphere of theology. A worthy spokesman with whom to start, since he expresses the outlook of many high-minded humanists, is the late Professor Gilbert Murray. He once stated, in an autobiographical note:

My reaction towards the traditional religion of the society in which I was born began early as a moral rebellion in early childhood. I began in my teens to be uneasy about other elements in the New Testament . . . including the concept of vicarious atonement.[7]

A similar outlook was expressed by a one time president of the British Humanist Association, Barbara Smoker, who declared:

Why do I hate the god I don't believe in? Because it is a grotesque distortion of all ideas of morality to think that a god can be all powerful, all good, and yet allow such horror in the world.

In the same context she added that one such horror was vicarious atonement, or in her own words, that 'he died for us, is a moral outrage'.[8]

Lest it be imagined that these intellectual difficulties are confined to English humanists, I will quote from writers of mainland Europe as well. The French anthropologist René Girard has made an extensive study of primitive religion, and particularly of their sacrifices, and he has expressed his own sentiments as follows:

Sacrifice has often been described as an act of mediation between the sacrificer and the deity. Because the very concept of deity, much less deity who receives blood sacrifices has little reality in this day and age, the entire institution of sacrifice is relegated by most modern theorists to the realm of the imagination.[9]

Elsewhere the same writer expressed himself even more strongly when commenting on the medieval theology of sacrifice:

God feels the need to revenge his honour, which has been tainted by the sins of humanity, and so on. Not only does God require a new victim, but he requires the victim who is most precious and dear to him, his very own son. No doubt this line of reasoning has done more than anything else to discredit christianity in the eyes of people of good will in the modern world.[10]

For the sake of completeness, one should bear in mind that coming to terms with the crucifixion, and all the savagery which it implies, is not confined to non-believers. The Catholic theologian Hans Küng has described graphically the attitude of the modern mind, both believer and atheist, when faced with the idea of the sacrifice of Christ. To quote his own words:

Since in modern man's environment cultic sacrifices are no longer offered, and there is no need to point to a Christian sacrifice in defending the faith against pagans . . . the concept of sacrifice is not related to any experience and has thus become largely misleading and unintelligible.[11]

(Pointing to a Christian sacrifice was a necessity in the patristic period when the Christians had to make it clear that they had not abolished one of the staple elements of religion. In a similar way they had to defend themselves against the charge of atheism because their monotheism gave the impression that they had diminished the number of deities in the universe.)

Bearing in mind the various categories of people for whom the crucifixion presents a greater or lesser difficulty in their deepest convictions about life, I have decided to address this book to mainstream believers, in many Churches, for whom the crucifixion of Jesus is a serious difficulty. That is to say, for people who believe in a loving God, and who find it exceedingly difficult to reconcile this understanding of their deity with one who would require the cruel death of Jesus.

In the preceding pages I have touched upon the subjects of original sin, evil, and grace, in order to establish the context for this present enquiry. I will say no more about them except to remind the reader that they are all interconnected, and at the centre of them we come back constantly to the work of the atonement: that is to say, the cause by which evil was counteracted, and the human race was reconciled to God the Father. It is to that problem alone that I confine my attention in the chapters which follow.

NOTES

(When citing foreign books, I will refer to English translations where it is feasible.)

1 Thomas Aquinas, *Summa Theologiae* (hereafter referred to as ST) III, q. 48, a. 2, ad 1.
2 Raymund Schwager, *Brauchen wir einen Sündenbock?* (2nd edition; Munich, 1986).
3 When I refer to the human race I will try to employ inclusive language. If I employ masculine words, it is simply a matter of convenience, as I do not

wish to burden the text with pedantic circumlocutions which interrupt the flow of the words. Clearly both sexes are involved in the economy of salvation, and the context will invariably make it clear where masculine pronouns are used in a universalist sense.

4 Jürgen Moltmann, *Theology of Hope* (London, 1967), pp. 34, 35, 225, 229.
5 Ceslaus Spicq, *Théologie morale du Nouveau Testament* (Paris, 1965), vol. I, p. 353.
6 Quoted in Hans Küng, *Global Responsibility* (London, 1991), p. 2.
7 From the preface to Gilbert Murray, *Stoic, Christian, Humanist*, quoted in Duncan Wilson's biography *Gilbert Murray* (Oxford, 1987), p. 398.
8 Quoted in *The Guardian* (28 July 1988), p. 16.
9 René Girard, *Violence and the Sacred* (Baltimore and London, 1979), p. 6.
10 René Girard, *Things Hidden Since the Foundation of the World* (Baltimore and London, 1987), p. 182.
11 Hans Küng, *On Being a Christian* (London, 1977), p. 425.

2

⊠ *The execution of Jesus*

At a superficial level the average person has some idea of sacrifice and atonement, as can be seen from a newspaper report in 1989. Two years previously a South Korean airliner had exploded in flight, killing all the passengers and crew. A North Korean agent was arrested, and when she was on trial she told the court in Seoul

that she wanted to die to atone for her role in planting a bomb on the South Korean airliner in 1987 that killed all 115 people on board. 'I feel like dying to atone for what I did', Kim Hyon-hui, aged 27, said. The prosecutor has demanded the death sentence.[1]

On reflection it becomes clear that ideas about sacrifice and atonement, such as are implied by the previous paragraph, can be seriously misleading. They are strongly influenced by concepts retained from a badly understood Christian past, from psychology or from pagan religions, which could distort the refined and precise concepts of the New Testament. Christian popular piety has also a great deal to answer for in the trivialization of the atonement, owing to the tone of pious hyperbole in countless poor-quality hymns and prayers. These have been sung and recited so often that they have become part of the intellectual furniture of the Christian mind, and perhaps of the whole of society. At this early stage in our enquiry it is imperative to ask ourselves what exactly does the New Testament have to say about the death of Jesus? To what extent was it a sacrifice, and in what sense? What was its causative role (if any) in the work of the atonement?

This will require some clarifications. First of all it was nothing like the popular notion epitomized by the North Korean agent. Christ had no personal guilt to be purged. Secondly, if sacrificial language is used or implied, what did the writers of the New

Testament understand thereby? In recent years the phenomenon of sacrifice has been studied extensively by anthropologists and specialists in comparative religion. Their writings are readily available.[2] However one may well hesitate before interpreting the New Testament's use of sacrificial language in the light of pagan religions. Admittedly the most primitive accounts of sacrifice in the ancient period of Israelite history did undoubtedly share the religious presuppositions of their pagan neighbours. Yet during the period of more than a thousand years their religious ideas were refined in the long formative pilgrimage which gave them, about the time of Jesus, a religious outlook which was totally different from that of the people in neighbouring countries. Not only was their monotheism utterly distinctive, but also their understanding of their relationship with God.

For these reasons I prefer to leave to one side the ideas on sacrifice as found in non-Jewish religions. If the writers of the New Testament use sacrificial language about the death of Jesus, their concepts will undoubtedly have been formed by their own exclusive religious tradition, and in particular by the understanding of sacrifice which was current in late Judaism. Therefore I intend to make use of the analysis of sacrifice elaborated by Roland de Vaux, in the light of his explanation of the matter as presented in the final compilation of the biblical books.[3] He maintains that the essential elements of sacrifice are the giving of a gift to God by the worshipper as a sign of loyalty. Its destruction denotes that the gift is irrevocable. When it takes place in a holy place it signifies its transference to the invisible world. Eating a part signifies union with God, and if the element of expiation is present it denotes yet another aspect of the relationship with the divinity, namely the quest for reconciliation.

The next clarification relates to the previous one. The violent death of Jesus was so devastating for his followers that some rationalization of it had to be found. After two thousand years of Christian history we take it for granted that it was a positive and creative achievement. The earliest Christian community had no such reassurance. The execution of the Messiah was so shattering for them that some explanation had to be worked out to enable them to come to terms with it. At one level his death could be viewed as martyrdom, and as the persecution during the Maccabean period was still present in their memory this idea would not have been difficult to arrive at.

To take the matter one stage further and explain his death as a sacrifice would have come more easily to that generation than to ours, in view of the central role which sacrifice played in all religions of that epoch. However, although sacrificial ideas would have come to mind quite readily, we must ask with considerable care, how far and with what limitations did they apply to the death of Jesus words and images culled from the liturgical practice of the Jerusalem Temple?

With these considerations in mind we can turn to the pages of the New Testament to investigate precisely how they interpreted the death of Jesus as a sacrifice, and what causative role they attributed to it.

As is well known, the idea of a sacrificial death is prominent in the epistles, but not in the synoptic gospels, and it is strongly implied in the imagery of the writings of St John. This distribution should not surprise us. The synoptics record mainly the teachings of Jesus, principally about the Kingdom of God, and in any case his execution had not taken place during the period to which they accord most coverage. By contrast the other New Testament writings represent a further stage in theological reflection, and elaborate all that was entailed in the salvific force which had been let loose in the world by God.

In various places primitive catechetical formulae have been preserved, as in 1 Corinthians 15:3: 'For I delivered to you as of first importance what I also received, that Christ died for our sins in accordance with the Scriptures.' This is the simplest formulation of the notion which received greater elaboration elsewhere in the Pauline letters and other writings of the New Testament.

The role of God the Father is clear, but being relatively simple, does not command lengthy commentary. The author of the salvific plan was not Christ, but the Father, and it is on his initiative that the Son was sent into the world to liberate it (cf. 2 Thessalonians 2:13, 14; Galatians 4:4). This perspective implies three ages in the spiritual history of the human race. The first being up to the time of Moses, when there was no revealed Law, and sin was not imputed. The second stage lasted from Moses to Christ, when the Law had been given and when sin and guilt were imputed. In the final stage Christ had brought an end to the Law and all that went with it. This is what lies behind the message of Ephesians 2:14–16:

For he is our peace, who has made us both one and has broken down the dividing wall of hostility, by abolishing in his flesh the law of commandments and ordinances, that he might create in himself one new man in the place of the two, so making peace, and might reconcile us both to God in one body through the cross, thereby bringing the hostility to an end.

The role of the Son receives more extensive treatment from St Paul. Starting with formulae from the infant Church's catechesis he elaborated a profound explanation of the death of Jesus showing his readers in what way it was a sacrifice, which freed us from the effects of evil. Within the limits of this book, I must assume that the reader is aware of the pre-existence and divinity of the Son as second person of the Trinity.[4] The passion, death, and resurrection of Jesus were decisive in overcoming sin. He does not employ the modern technical term 'cause', but the concept is present by implication as he describes the events and their results.

The concept of Christ dying for our sins occurs frequently in the Pauline letters (cf. 1 Corinthians 1:13; Romans 14:15; Galatians 1:4 and 3:13; 2 Corinthians 5:14, 21; Ephesians 5:2). I mention all these instances to make it clear that the thought is constant in his letters, and not just an isolated phrase. It makes no difference whether he uses the phrase 'for us' or 'for our sins', since the underlying sense is the same.

The unambiguous use of the word sacrifice for the death of Jesus occurs in Ephesians 5:2. Actually two technical terms are used which leave the matter in no possible doubt: 'Christ loves us and gave himself up for us, a fragrant offering (*prosphoran*) and sacrifice (*thusian*) to God.' No specific kind of sacrifice is mentioned there (unlike Hebrews and the writings of St John, where the precise type of sacrifice is always clear). Occasionally St Paul is precise on the point as in 1 Corinthians 11:25: 'This cup is the New Covenant in my blood.' It is the passage in which he is recounting the Last Supper, and the sacrifice which he had in mind was that with which Moses inaugurated the Old Covenant on Mount Sinai.

The connection with sin is made explicit in a couple of other places. Firstly 2 Corinthians 5:21, which is puzzling: 'For our sake he made him to be sin (*hamartian*) who knew no sin (*hamartian*) so that in him we might become the righteousness of God.' Most probably it is to be understood that Christ became a sin offering, since in Hebrew the two words are the same. Its meaning is thus clear, but it is uncharacteristic of St Paul, and Bultmann is probably right when he says that it is an echo of pre-Pauline catechesis.

A similar attribution to Christ of a technical term related to sin offerings is to be found in Romans 3:24, 25: 'they are justified by his grace, as a gift, through the redemption which is in Christ Jesus, whom God put forward as an expiation *(hilastērion)* by his blood.' In St Paul's vocabulary the technical word *hilastērion* has two meanings: either it can denote that an object has become ritually pure, or it can be used as the equivalent of *kapporet*, which is the Hebrew name for the gold plate on top of the Ark of the Covenant. On the festival of the Day of Atonement the high priest was directed, in Leviticus, to pour the blood of the victim on that gold plate.

I will have more to say about the liturgy of the Day of Atonement when I discuss the Letter to the Hebrews. For the moment I wish simply to warn against a premature simplification as if compensation were being offered to an angry god. Secular Greek uses the term *hilastērion* to mean compensation, and in this sense it is found three times in the Septuagint (Malachi 1:9; Zechariah 7:2, 8:22). Yet in none of these three instances is there any question of placating God's anger. The Jewish understanding of the sin offering was a more elevated notion than that of appeasing the rage of a bloodthirsty deity. According to Leviticus 17:11 (which is one of the few places in the Old Testament which offers any kind of explanation of the mechanism of sacrifice), the blood contains the life. When the priest poured the victim's blood on to the *kapporet* he was symbolically transferring the life to the divine realm as a quasi-possession of God. In the present instance of its occurrence in Romans 3:25 it implies that Christ poured out his own blood on the cross, which had taken on the role of the *kapporet*. The readers who were familiar with the liturgy of the Day of Atonement would have grasped the significance straight away, namely that Christ's blood had achieved perfectly what the annual sacrifice of the Day of Atonement had been prefiguring.

At this stage of our enquiry it is important to realize that St Paul did not limit the atoning work of Jesus simply to his violent death. E. Schillebeeckx declared that the whole life of Christ from conception to the Ascension was redemptive.[5] I will say a great deal more about this at a later stage of the book. For the moment I would like to draw the reader's attention to the role of the resurrection which is also, in the writings of St Paul, an integral

part of the work of human liberation from sin and its consequences, and which was seriously neglected until the modern re-
birth of biblical theology. The most succinct expression of this
dimension of the work of Christ is in Romans 4:25: '. . . Jesus our
Lord who was put to death for our trespasses and raised for our
justification.' It was in virtue of this that he was named the Saviour
(*Sōtēr*). This term is rare in St Paul, occurring only in Philippians
3:20 and Ephesians 5:23, possibly because it was employed in
secular Greek usage for pagan gods and for the Roman emperors.

The effects of Christ's liberating work are expressed in a variety
of different ways. The basic notion of reconciliation between God
the Father and the human race occurs in various places. Perhaps
2 Corinthians 5:18–20 is the clearest:

> All this is from God who through Christ reconciled us to himself and gave us
> the ministry of reconciliation; that is, in Christ, God was reconciling the world
> to himself, not counting their trespasses against them, and entrusting to us the
> message of reconciliation.

Expiation of sins is stated in Ephesians 5:2, 25, but the stress is on
love, rather than on anger. Liberation too is spelt out as in 1
Corinthians 6:20 where the word 'purchased' is used, though from
whom the purchase was made is not mentioned. The same silence
is to be seen in the Old Testament passages relating to the Exodus.
The Israelites were said to have been purchased: the purchaser was
named as God, but the identity of the vendor is never stated. It is
an implied contention that neither the Egyptians nor the devil has
genuine rights over God's chosen people.

The interior effect on the believer is usually termed justification, which for simplicity's sake could be described as becoming
morally acceptable to God. (So much has been written on this
particular matter in the theology of grace that I will refer my
readers to the standard textbooks and devote no further space to it
here.)

Before turning to the period before St Paul wrote his letters and
trying to investigate the origin of the ideas which he developed, it
is important to give some consideration to the Letter to the
Hebrews.[6]

The author of this letter presupposes in his readers a detailed
knowledge of the Jerusalem Temple and its liturgy, about which he
writes with perceptible nostalgia, although he declares that it had
outlived its purpose by the time that he was writing. He writes

extensively about the death of Jesus, but for the moment I will limit my observations to his theologizing on the matter in the terms of the ritual of the Day of Atonement. This was an annual festival, when in accordance with the prescriptions in Leviticus[7] the high priest selected two goats as victims. One was driven out into the wilderness beyond the city walls, symbolically taking with it the sins of the people.

The other animal was killed and its blood was poured on to the *kapporet* in the inner sanctuary. After that the high priest entered into the Holy of Holies to pray for the people. This was the innermost part of the sanctuary (the tabernacle in the days of wandering, and later in the Temple). The high priest alone was allowed to enter there, and he did so only once a year, on the occasion of this festival. It is worth mentioning that this was the place where the Israelites' neighbours placed the statues of their deities, in temples of similar design. For the Israelites, though, the space was empty, being considered as the dwelling place of the name of the true God who could not be depicted in any material way. When the Romans eventually conquered Palestine, the Roman general Pompey forced his way in there despite the vehement protests of the Jewish priests, and he was astonished to find it empty.

In chapter 9 of Hebrews the author describes how the death of Jesus fulfilled what had been prefigured in that liturgy. From 9:11 onwards we read:

But when Christ appeared as the high priest of the good things which have come, then through the greater and more perfect tent (not made with hands, that is, not of this creation) he entered once for all into the Holy Place taking not the blood of goats and calves, but his own blood, thus securing an eternal redemption. For if the sprinkling of defiled persons with the blood of goats and bulls and with the ashes of a heifer sanctifies for the purification of the flesh, how much more shall the blood of Christ, who through the eternal spirit offered himself without blemish to God, purify your conscience from dead works to serve the living God.

Both in the passage just quoted and in other parts of Hebrews it is clear that the author regards the death of Jesus as a true sacrifice, and the removal of sins and their effects is expressedly attributed to this *thusia*.[8] Unlike the pagans the Jews did not think in terms of placating the anger of a bloodthirsty deity. During the course of many centuries prior to the writing of this letter their understanding of their relationship with God had enabled them to think of sin and reconciliation in more sophisticated terms. Generally the Old Testament did not speak of sin as offending God, but of preventing him from showing his favour. Remission of sins in this perspective was spoken of in a variety of refined but graphic metaphors. It was said that God closed his eyes to the sins (Wisdom 12:23), or that he threw the sins behind him (Isaiah 38:17), that he trampled them underfoot (Micah 7:19), covered them so that they were not seen (Psalm 85:3; Nehemiah 3:37), no longer imputed them to the sinner (Numbers 12:11; Job 7:21), or that he didn't remember them any more (Ezekiel 33:16). [9]

Hebrews implies that the Jews considered that the ritual of the Day of Atonement was efficacious (to use a modern term anachronistically). The author of the letter is emphatic that it was not effective, and that the sacrifice of Jesus alone was. The precise mechanism by which this sacrifice attained its intended result is not spelt out in the letter. Its whole tenor implies that it was something to do with the personal perfection of Christ, but is no more explicit than that. In his commentary, at Hebrews 9:12, Spicq suggests a partial explanation that 'the line of thought implies that the value of the blood depends upon the value of the person who sheds it'. [10] Perhaps I am being unfair, but I seem to detect there some overtones of Anselm's theory of satisfaction, about which I will say more in Chapter 4.

In conclusion to this brief examination of Hebrews and the letters of St Paul, I think that it is fair to say that the execution of Jesus was theologized as an expiatory sacrifice bringing to perfection the Old Testament sacrifices which had been inefficacious prefigurations of it. [11]

We are now in a position to ask ourselves more precisely about the origin of the notion of an atoning death, or expiatory sacrifice. Granted that it is central to the epistles and especially to St Paul, we must ask: did he invent it, or did he derive it from elsewhere?

To some extent the notion of an atoning death was part of the general cultural background of St Paul's readership. It is superfluous to dwell upon the fact that his letters were written for converts among the Jews of the Diaspora, and for erstwhile pagans, for whom the international language and culture were Greek. For them the idea of a death to placate the wrath of the gods was almost commonplace. Classical literature has countless examples. [12] On this matter Martin Hengel has written:

In this context it is particularly striking how many contacts can be demonstrated between ancient Greek ideas and those of the Old Testament . . . the inhabitants of the Mediterranean world would not find it difficult to understand Christ's death as an atoning sacrifice.[13]

He also states that the Christian message was distinctive in many respects, not least because it was claimed that the death of Christ was for the atonement of all human guilt, a claim which had never been made *à propos* of any other atoning death.[14]

In addition to what the Greek world picture had to offer, the religious consciousness of late Judaism had a further distinctive component to contribute to this complex of ideas, namely the vicarious atonement achieved in the death of a martyr. In the literature of the inter-testamental period there are a number of passages which speak of the deaths of Jewish martyrs which would now be described as vicarious atonement. The earliest piece of evidence is probably 2 Maccabees 7:33. The book is difficult to date, but it was almost certainly earlier than St Paul's writings.[15] In the narrative of the deaths of the seven brothers in the Seleucid persecution, the last one says, just before his own execution: 'We are suffering for our own sins; and if to punish and discipline us, our living Lord vents his wrath upon us, he will yet be reconciled with his own servants.' Concerning this passage we can say at least, that the shedding of the martyrs' blood involved the cessation of the divine wrath against Israel.[16] Basically this was an act of vicarious atonement. The idea is spelt out more positively in other writings of the same period, as for example in the non-canonical Fourth Book of Maccabees. In the description which is given of the martyrdom of Eleazar, he is reported as saying, just before his death: 'Be merciful unto thy people, and let our punishment be a satisfaction in their behalf. Make my blood their purification, and take my soul to ransom their souls.'[17] The precise rendering of the Semitic words which lie behind 'soul' is always a problem for translators, since what is designated is the whole living person. However this point does not alter the fact that in this passage the theology of vicarious atonement is clear, and it is expressed in specifically sacrificial language.

The same clarity of thought can be seen later in the same book where the author is reflecting more generally on the deaths of all the martyrs of that period. In 4 Maccabees 17:21 we read:

And these men therefore, having sanctified themselves for God's sake, not only have received this honour but also the honour that through them the enemy had no more power over our people, and the tyrant suffered punishment, and our country was purified, they having as it were become a ransom for our nation's sin; and through the blood of these righteous men and the propitiation of their death, the divine providence delivered Israel that before was evil entreated.[18]

Once again the dating of this book is not easy. It seems reasonable to assign it to the first half of the first century AD.[19]

A somewhat more subtle indication of the same line of thought can be detected in the Greek translation of the Book of Daniel. It is now recognized that ancient translators of the Bible sometimes acted with a degree of freedom which would shock modern practitioners of the same art. As they undertook their task at varying lengths of time after the composition of the originals, they were the beneficiaries of more highly developed theological thinking. From time to time they seem to have felt at liberty to introduce their more up-to-date insights into the ancient texts which they were translating. One such instance can be seen when Daniel was rendered into Greek. In 3:28 of the Septuagint version we read concerning the torment of Azariah and his companions in the fiery furnace: 'So may our sacrifice be before you this day to bring about atonement with thee (*exilasai opisthen sou*).'

It would be unwise to erect too large a theoretical superstructure upon the foundation of a few texts, but it cannot be denied that these writers indicate a climate of opinion, namely that among some of the contemporaries of Jesus, the notion of the vicarious atoning value of a martyr's death would not have been unknown or alien to Jewish religious thinking of that period.[20]

Having set the scene and described the theological and cultural context within which the notion of an atoning death would not have been alien or misunderstood, it is now time to pursue our enquiry more precisely into the origins and exact meaning of the formulae which are employed in the New Testament when speaking of the death of Jesus. The basic formulae are to be found in Romans. In 8:32 we read: 'He who did not spare his own son, but gave him up for us all.' This phrase is strongly suggestive of the giving up of Isaac by Abraham in Genesis 22:12. However a more theologically sophisticated source can be located. Before examining it, one should also look at the double phrase in Romans 4:25:

'Jesus our Lord who was put to death for our trespasses and raised for our justification.'

It seems reasonable to locate the origin of 'give up *(paradidomai)*' in chapter 53 of Isaiah, where the word occurs three times, and where the context is that of the Servant dying for other people's spiritual benefit. Because of its importance and relevance to the present enquiry I will quote at length from that particular chapter of Isaiah. The first part of the chapter describes the sufferings of the Servant and from verse 5 onwards the writer becomes more specific about the significance of his afflictions:

(v. 5) But he was wounded for our transgressions, he was bruised for our iniquities; upon him was the chastisement that made us whole, and with his stripes we are healed. (v. 6) All we like sheep have gone astray; we have turned every one to his own way; and the Lord has laid on him *(paredōken auton)* the iniquity of us all. (v. 7) He was oppressed and he was afflicted, yet he opened not his mouth; like a lamb that is led to the slaughter, and like a sheep that before its shearer is dumb, so he opened not his mouth. (v. 8) By oppression and judgement he was taken away; and as for his generation, who considered that he was cut off out of the land of the living, stricken for the transgression of my people? (v. 9) And they made his grave with the wicked and with a rich man in his death, although he had done no violence, and there was no deceit in his mouth. (v. 10) Yet it was the will of the Lord to bruise him; he has put him to grief; when he makes himself an offering for sin, he shall see his offspring, he shall prolong his days; the will of the Lord shall prosper his hand; (v. 11) he shall see the fruit of the travail of his soul and be satisfied; by his knowledge shall the righteous one my servant, make many to be accounted righteous; and he shall bear their iniquities. (v. 12) Therefore I will divide him a portion with the great, and he shall divide the spoil with the strong; because he poured out his soul to death *(paredothē eis thanaton hē psychē)*, and was numbered with the transgressors; yet he bore the sins of many, and made intercession for the transgressors *(dia tas hamartias autōn paredothē)*.

It is significant that the concept of suffering on account of other people's sins, with a view to bringing about some sort of remedy (albeit imprecise), is expressed in a variety of ways, and is not confined to any one technical phrase.

A glance through the standard commentaries on Isaiah will indicate that exegetes find no difficulty in recognizing that an expiatory sacrifice is being referred to in that chapter.[21] Bonnard in his commentary draws attention to the significant fact that the Servant is spoken of as bearing the sins of many (in effect therefore of everyone), whereas in the past the people of the Old Testament were accustomed to bearing the consequences only of their own sins, or those of their fathers.[22]

One further precision is needed in our examination of the concept of the Servant being 'given up'. There is no indication in pre-Christian Judaism that Isaiah 53 was understood as foreseeing a suffering Messiah. That identification must have been the innovative work of the early Christian community in their efforts to come to an understanding of the crucifixion of Jesus.

Granted that the wording of the key phrases was inspired by the Old Testament and particularly by Isaiah 53, we have yet to ask when the creative work took place in the formulation of these crucial theological concepts. A key text is 1 Corinthians 15:3–4:

For I delivered to you as of first importance what I also received, that Christ died for our sins in accordance with the Scriptures, that he was buried, and that he was raised on the third day in accordance with the Scriptures.

It is generally agreed that this represents the pre-Pauline tradition. It is part of the message which Paul handed on to the people of Corinth when he founded the community there probably in the winter of AD 49–50. We know that other Christian missionaries went there too, including St Peter in the period between the initial evangelization and the writing of the first letter. At the end of the passage (verse 11) it is indicated that they too preached the same message. It seems reasonable therefore to trace the origin of the idea, and the wording, to a time before St Paul's mission to Corinth, and the Antioch community at the time of his conversion would be the obvious source.[23]

The concise formulae of the early Church's catechesis contain three closely related, but distinct ideas, namely that the Messiah was given up for execution, that the precise form of death was crucifixion, and that his death was an act of vicarious atonement. After two thousand years of Christian history and theological reflection we take these ideas for granted. It requires a great effort of imagination to step back and appreciate just how original and innovative these ideas were. Having traced the insights and their technical formulae back to the pre-Pauline community at Antioch, we are in a position to ask ourselves whether we can pursue the investigation further and trace, with some degree of probability, their precise origin.

Returning for a moment to 1 Corinthians 15:3, let us examine the expression 'Christ died'. It does not say that the man Jesus died, but precisely that it was the Messiah who died (since the English word 'Christ' is a transliteration of the Greek translation of *Messiah* in Hebrew). Elsewhere in St Paul's letters it is clear that the death (as is well known) had been by crucifixion. The notion of a crucified Messiah was so alien to Jewish expectations, that the phrase must be construed as a virtual blasphemy in the time of St Paul. It is not the kind of expression which would have arisen haphazardly. In fact one can regard it as a classical instance of the criterion of dissimilarity. The notion was so much at variance with current sentiment and expectations of the Messiah's contemporaries that it must have been forced upon them by facts and circumstances which could not be ignored. In short the very *titulus* which was attached to the cross of Jesus (Mark 15:26 and parallels) made the conjunction of ideas inescapable.[24]

As to the atoning value of the death of Jesus: how far back can that idea be traced with any degree of probability? It is now widely accepted that the gospels represent varying degrees of theological reflection, by the communities and evangelists, on the words and deeds of Jesus. To say that they were written after the earliest epistles raises as many questions as it solves, since their composition must have been a complex process of reflection and the crystallization of ideas dating back to the first years after the resurrection. Nor was the writing of them as simple as that of the epistles which were composed in one operation. The gospels must have gone through an oral phase when certain parts received a stereotyped form thanks to their being memorized exactly. It is almost certain that these same sections were written down as separate units prior to their inclusion in the final form of the gospels as we have them today. During the course of this complex process the theological significance of the events and their elaboration was being developed.

Having said all that, it would be a gross oversimplification to ascribe all the theologically significant phrases to the creative work of the early community, as if to suggest that Jesus himself was incapable of any such reflective activity. Nevertheless the whole operation of exploring the origin of the atoning sacrifice is a delicate one, and rests upon the careful weighting of probabilities.

There are only two instances in the words of Jesus where he speaks of his own death as a sacrifice, namely at the Last Supper, and in the saying, 'For the son of man came not to be served but to serve, and to give his life as a ransom for many (*lutron anti pollōn*)'

(Mark 10:45; Matthew 20:28). Some years ago it was fairly common to take for granted the fact that this expression would not have been used by Jesus, but that the evangelists took it from St Paul and placed the words on the lips of Jesus. With the passage of time and the progress of scholarship that extreme position now commands less confidence. Personally I see no insuperable difficulty in attributing the words to Jesus himself. Admittedly the notion of an atoning death is rare in the gospels. This is because they were mainly concerned to record his teaching, which was principally about the Kingdom of Heaven, and all that went with it, and quite simply because his death had not taken place during the period to which they devoted the most extensive coverage. It is natural that anticipatory theological reflection upon his violent death (albeit foreseen) should be relatively rare in his teaching. A. Richardson has pointed out that Paul would be an unlikely source for the expression 'ransom for many' since the word *lutron* does not occur in his letters.[25] E. Lohse goes one stage further. While agreeing that *lutron* does not occur in the Pauline letters, he points out that the expression 'for the many' is absent too. The phrase is clearly of Palestinian origin, all of which makes it clear that the evangelists did not lift it from St Paul.[26] A similar conclusion is arrived at by an even later author: H. I. Marshall states that the phrase in Mark 10:45 represents the simplest form of the redemptive concept and is 'undoubtedly from the earliest tradition of the Church, and there are good reasons to argue that it is an authentic saying of Jesus'.[27] Schillebeeckx too presented more or less the same judgement:

As it turns out therefore the soteriological formulae form a very old and self-contained complex of tradition, the emergence of which cannot be accounted for either by secondary deduction from other interpretations of Jesus' death or by referring it to Jewish theologies of the martyrs' vicarious sufferings.[28]

The likelihood that Jesus himself pronounced the phrase is strengthened by the fact that he used an expression very like the crucial *lutron* when he was speaking about the end of the world. The end of ordinary history is spoken of as redemption for his followers: 'Now when these things begin to take place, look up and raise your heads, because your redemption (*apolutrōsis*) is drawing near' (Luke 21:28). Furthermore the expression 'ransom for many' has Semitic overtones, which suggests that it was translated from Aramaic or Hebrew. This points to an Aramaic-speaking community, if not to the words of Jesus himself.[29]

Fortunately the account of the last supper has been recorded in four places, the three synoptics and St Paul, and their near unanimity is important.[30] St Paul states, what its literary form confirms, that his narrative of the event was part of the early community's catechesis, which he had received as a neophyte and presumably memorized. In spite of that the wording in Paul and Luke indicates a small advance in theological reflection over the other two, insofar as the blessing of the cup specifies that it is the new covenant: 'This cup is the new covenant in my blood.' This is an unmistakable allusion to the new covenant which had been foretold in the prophecy of Jeremiah 31:31. The accounts in Mark and Matthew leave that detail to be inferred. All four accounts clearly reflect the sacrifice which accompanied the Sinai covenant as recorded in Exodus 24:8. What is interesting for our particular enquiry is that the Aramaic targums of that chapter of Exodus (both Onkelos and Yerushalmi I) had interpreted the sacrifice which went with the Sinai covenant as being an atoning sacrifice for the sins of the people. This detail is important because it is one more indication that the notion of an atoning sacrifice was part of the theological consciousness among the contemporaries of Jesus, which further undermines the allegation that such an idea could not have been in the mind or on the lips of Jesus.

As to the exact source of the insight that Jesus was instituting the commemoration of his own atoning death, Jeremias has drawn attention to the fact that the Passover supper provided the ideal opportunity for theological explanation.[31] It was customary every year at the Passover meal for the eldest son to ask his father the formalized question 'What is the meaning of this night?' The father than explained, year after year, the narrative of the Exodus and the deliverance of the Israelite ancestors from Egypt. When Jesus celebrated the meal for the last time with his apostles someone in the group would have posed that question, and Jesus as their leader would have had the perfect opportunity to explain his intentions with regard to his death which he knew was imminent.

In this way we trace the crucial ideas back to Jesus himself. In other words we can safely ascribe to Jesus the theological evaluation of his death as being an atoning sacrifice. In fact it is inconceivable that something as central as the eucharist (and all that went with it) should have been invented, and placed upon the lips of Jesus by the catechesis of the early Church. Put in another way we can say that if the institution of the eucharist is not accepted as deriving directly from Jesus himself, then nothing else in the gospels could be taken as authentic.

One final link in the chain needs to be forged, and that is to try and conjecture how the early community so quickly grasped and appreciated the significance of Christ's death being an atoning sacrifice. This part of the investigation is indeed conjectural because one has to penetrate behind the written records to the period when the tradition was in its oral and formative phase. I follow here the speculations of Martin Hengel, who himself states that his ideas are hypothetical to some extent.

The basic problem is that habitually the apostles were slow to grasp the significance of what Jesus was trying to convey to them. The gospels are full of such instances. Indeed at the Last Supper itself, the harmony and solemnity of the occasion was marred by an infantile quarrel about seniority as implied by the assigning of places at the table. In spite of that tendency, they grasped very quickly the significance of the death of the Master.

The first stage was presumably that Jesus himself, in advance of the event, interpreted his own death as a sacrifice in terms of Isaiah 53, and in the light of the sacrifice which accompanied the first covenant at Sinai. Then, after the resurrection the apostles experienced the first consequences of the death of Jesus, namely their own forgiveness for their cowardice when in their various ways nearly all of them denied and abandoned him.

The next stage would most probably have been the results of the weekly celebration of the eucharist which would have provided them with the opportunity to reflect upon the death and resurrection of Jesus, and to ponder its implications. The resurrection confirmed that he was indeed the true Messiah, in spite of his having been crucified, and the notion of an atoning death for all the human race made the death itself intelligible and indeed supremely meaningful.[32] Hengel himself admits that this theory is somewhat conjectural, but it does give a coherent account of how the notion became so widely appreciated before the time of St Paul.

In conclusion to this chapter, it can be said that a brief examination of the New Testament evidence indicates that the writers did indeed regard the death of Jesus as a sacrifice, and that it had a causal role in the atonement. They do not confine the causality to the actual death, because the resurrection too is presented as a part of the process. What else entered in as well I will discuss in Chapter 6. Although the authors of the various epistles devoted much thought to the theological elaboration of the saving death, it is reasonable to regard them as not having created the notion. The basic ideas can prudently be traced back to the teaching of Jesus himself.

One final word needs to be said. There is no attempt in the New Testament to explain the causality behind the work of liberating the human race from sin. Jews and pagans at that time regarded sacrifices as being efficacious (to use a modern word anachronistic-ally), and it would have been alien to their intellectual perspectives to have enquired further into the causal process. In this respect the authors of the New Testament did not advance beyond the limitations of their predecessors in the Old Testament. Since the present book is concerned principally with that very question, namely what was the actual cause of the atonement, and how it operated, it may be useful to close this chapter by quoting on that matter the judgement of one of the most recent writers on the subject. 'The Old Testament offers no proper theory as to how the act of sacrifice could remove sin and guilt from the community or from individuals.'[33] Perhaps the nearest hint is to be found in Leviticus 17:11 which gives directions about the blood of sacrificial victims: ' . . . to make atonement for your souls; for it is the blood which makes atonement by reason of life.' The ancient Israelites considered that the life of animals and humans was indeed in the blood, but the sentence from Leviticus, which seemed to be on the verge of offering an explanation, merely pushes it one stage further back.

As the question of causality is the most pressing for the modern mind I will pursue it with increasing precision in the chapters which follow, indicating just how widespread was the failure to find a solution to this problem not only in the writers of antiquity, but among modern authors too.

NOTES

1 Reported in *The Guardian* (5 April 1989).
2 The bibliography on this subject is vast, so I will draw the reader's attention merely to a few standard works: E. O. James, *The Origins of Sacrifice* (London, 1933); H. Hubert and M. Mausse, *Sacrifice, Its Nature*

and Function (London, 1964); R. K. Yerkes, *Sacrifice in Greek and Roman Religions and Early Judaism* (London, 1953); E. O. James, *Seasonal Feasts and Festivals* (London, 1961); T. Linders and G. Nordquist, *Gifts to the Gods* (Uppsala, 1987).

3 R. de Vaux, *The Institutions of the Old Testament* (London, 1961), pp. 451–4.

4 The bibliography on this subject is beyond counting, but I would like to draw the reader's attention to two books of particular merit: L. Cerfaux, *Christ in the Theology of St Paul* (New York and London, 1959); A. Grillmeier, *Christ in Christian Tradition*, vol. I (London, 1965).

5 E. Schillebeeckx, *Christ the Sacrament of the Encounter with God* (London, 1963), p. 34.

6 In this section I am following closely the conclusions of C. Spicq, *Epître aux Hébreux* (2 vols, Paris, 1952, 1953).

7 Leviticus 16:1–34.

8 Hebrews 8:27; 9:23, 26.

9 Cf. Spicq, op. cit., vol. 1, p. 304, n.

10 Spicq, op. cit., vol. 2, p. 257.

11 L. Cerfaux, op. cit., pp. 143–7.

12 For a brief selection the following may be cited: Homer, *Iliad* I, 386, II, 550; *Odyssey* III, 419; Herodotus V, 47 and VII, 179; Pausanias III, 12, 13; Josephus, *Antiquities* VI, 124 and *Wars of the Jews* V, 19; Philo, *De Vita Mos.* II, 24 and *De Spec. Leg.* I, 116.

13 Martin Hengel, *The Atonement: The Origins of the Doctrine in the New Testament* (London, 1981), pp. 19 and 28.

14 Hengel, op. cit., p. 31.

15 J. Downing, 'Jesus and martyrdom', *Journal of Theological Studies* (1963), p. 280, cites the dates given by Eissfeldt (60 BC) and Zeitlin (AD 40).

16 Downing, art. cit., p. 283.

17 4 Maccabees 6:28, 29; in R. H. Charles, *Apocrypha and Pseudepigrapha of the Old Testament* (Oxford, 1963), vol. II, p. 674.

18 4 Maccabees 17:21, in Charles, op. cit., vol. II, p. 683.

19 Not later than AD 50 according to Lohse and about AD 40 according to Hadas; cf. Downing, art. cit., p. 80.

20 This conclusion is accepted not only by Downing (see above), but also by M. Hengel, op. cit., p. 61, and by Spicq, op. cit., vol. 2, p. 409.

21 C. Westermann, *Isaiah 40 – 60* (London, 1966), p. 269; E. J. Young, *The Book of Isaiah* (Grand Rapids, Michigan, 1972), vol. III, p. 358.

22 P. E. Bonnard, *Le Second Isaïe* (Paris, 1972), p. 286.

23 Cf. Hengel, op. cit., p. 36.

24 Hengel, op. cit., pp. 43–4.

25 A. Richardson, *Introduction to the Theology of the New Testament* (London, 1958), pp. 200–2.

26 E. Lohse, *Martyrer und Gottesknecht* (Göttingen, 1963), p. 117.

27 H. I. Marshall, *Jesus the Saviour* (London, 1990), p. 250.
28 E. Schillebeeckx, *Jesus* (London, 1979), p. 293.
29 Hengel, op. cit., p. 53.
30 1 Corinthians 11:23–25; Luke 21:14–20; Mark 24:22–25; Matthew 26:26–29.
31 J. Jeremias, *New Testament Theology* (London, 1971), vol. I, p. 290.
32 Hengel, op. cit., pp. 65ff.
33 P. S. Fiddes, *Past Event and Present Salvation: The Christian Idea of Atonement* (London, 1989), p. 68.

⊠ EXCURSUS TO CHAPTER 2
NO EXPLANATION: AGREED

Being reluctant to burden the main body of the text with too many quotations (and their attendant notes), and since they are ultimately of negative import, I have decided to gather together in this excursus a catena of modern writers. There is a consensus among them, which is something of a paradox in the context of this study, as they all agree that the New Testament does not tell us how the atonement was effected, yet they offer no explanation of it themselves to compensate for that omission. Ironically it is precisely this explanation which is so badly needed by the modern reader, who finds the violent death of Jesus so repugnant. The same audience desperately needs to be given a positive and cogent account of how humanity was liberated from sin, in order to make sense of an apparently senseless crucifixion. The intrinsic efficacy of sacrifices no longer convinces the modern mind, and contemporary enquirers are entitled to something satisfactory with which to replace the ancient convictions about blood offerings.

The selection which I offer is not exhaustive, but I trust that it is representative of the widespread consensus among theologians of different nations and Churches.

I will begin with Karl Barth, and I quote from the English translation of his *Church Dogmatics* (Edinburgh, 1956). In volume IV part 1, he speaks of the crucifixion and says of it

there is fulfilled in it the mission, the task, and the work of the Son of God, the reconciliation of the world with God. There takes place here the redemptive judgement of God on all men. To fulfil this judgement He took the place of all men, He took their place as sinners. In this passion there is legally re-established the covenant between God and man . . . (p. 247)

Later on in the same volume he speaks of the resurrection as the

fulfilment and proclamation of God's decision concerning the event of the cross. It is its acceptance as the act of the Son of God appointed our representative, an act which fulfilled the divine wrath. (p. 309)

Much the same is to be seen in volume IV part 2, about the incarnation, which was 'to fulfil the ineluctible judgement of God' (p. 4).

Nowhere does Barth explain how the reconciliation had been effected according to the mind of the New Testament writers, nor does he offer an explanation himself. Lest I seem ungenerous to so eminent a scholar as Barth I will add the views of two more recent commentators on his soteriology. The first is Raymund Schwager, writing an article entitled 'Der Richter wird gerichtet' in the *Zeitschrift für Katholische Theologie* (1985). On p. 125 he stated:

> The passion of Jesus Christ is, according to Barth, a divine action in the fullest sense, through which the evil in the world, and sin, were obliterated. Satisfaction occurred since the divine wrath could run its full course. The radical love is not the love based on cheap grace. It can achieve satisfaction only in the full realization of its wrath against sinful humanity, through death, abandonment and obliteration.

The second commentator on Barth is J. P. Galvin, writing an article entitled 'The marvellous exchange' in *The Thomist* (1989). On p. 686 he stated, *à propos* of Barth

> On the cross Christ is judged in our stead, in God's personal confrontation with evil. In bearing alone the sin of all, Christ overcame evil by allowing God's wrath to expend itself fully.

Both these commentators see in Barth the simple factual statement of the divine wrath being expended, as the only explanation of the causality of the atonement.

Vincent Taylor faced the same problem and was more explicit in acknowledging the lacuna in the New Testament's presentation of liberation. Speaking of Christ's death as reported in Hebrews he stated:

> the writer does not tell us how His offering avails for sinners in their approach to God. It may be thought of the offering as so complete in itself, and so immediately efficacious that no further explanation was necessary or even possible. (*The Atonement in New Testament Teaching* (London, 1940), p. 184)

He offered no explanation of his own.

After the Second World War H. E. W. Turner published his *Patristic Doctrine of the Redemption*, and in several places he had occasion to note how the Fathers understood the process by which the liberation from sin had been achieved. Here are a few examples. On p. 49 he wrote concerning the devil as the source of evil, 'Christ was successful in resisting the devil where Adam had been defeated'. On p. 95, concerning the quotation from 2 Peter about humans becoming partakers of the divine nature, he stated 'He became man in order that we may be deified'. The book contains other similar descriptions of the atoning work of Jesus.

All of them remain within the factual descriptive mode of the New Testament writers, and no deeper causal explanation is offered.

D. M. Baillie was concerned mainly with the incarnation in his book *God Was in Christ* (London, 1956), but he dealt with the atonement incidentally, as on p. 188 for instance:

If we take the christology of the New Testament at its highest, we can only say that 'God was in Christ' in that great atoning sacrifice, and even that the priest and the victim were none other than God. There is in the New Testament no uniformity of conception as to how this sacrifice brings about the reconciliation.

Nor did Baillie offer a theory of his own.

In 1967 J. J. Altizer published *The Gospel of Christian Atheism*, which affords an example of what could be called the preacher's paradox. The underlying thought in the book is that the revelation of God in the Old Testament was so artificial and remote that it concealed him from man, and that it was therefore an alienation. The crucifixion put an end to all of that, and by being the destruction of something negative, allowed the true nature of God to come through positively. On p. 113 Altizer states:

His death is a self negation or self annihilation: consequently, by freely willing the dissolution of his transcendent 'selfhood', the Godhead reverses the life and movement of the transcendent realm, transforming Transcendence into immanence, thereby abolishing the ground of every alien other.

The word 'abolishing' in the previous sentence is the closest which the author approaches to a causal explanation, but how that abolition was achieved is not explained.

Probably the most widely read and influential book on the atonement in the English-speaking world has been F. W. Dillistone's *Christian Understanding of the Atonement* (London, 1968). He speaks often of the causality of the sacrifice of Jesus, and points out clearly that the biblical authors offered no rational explanation of how it produced its effect, namely the moral liberation of the human race. I will quote first of all from his analysis of the Day of Atonement as presented in the Letter to the Hebrews:

Christ the high priest of a new order entered into heaven itself, once and for all, bearing his own life blood, to make adequate reconciliation for the sins of the whole world and for people of all ages. The 'how' of the purifying act is not a question for enquiry. (p. 140)

When speaking of sacrifice in the wider context of the religion of the Greeks and Romans he states

... infringements of obligations to the gods were atoned for by sacrifices, ... their efficacity did not depend on participation of peoples as a whole ... their effects were believed to accrue automatically by Law of Nature. (p. 177)

On the same page Dillistone turns again to the efficacity of sacrifices in the Israelite religion and states

When blood is applied by a priest to the most holy place of communion between God and man, any defect or defilement is deemed to be removed and the free communion or interflow of life with life is restored. The 'how' of this operation remains a mystery.

The mysterious effectiveness may have satisfied the ancients but it is not adequate for the climate of enquiry in the modern world.

Towards the end of the book, when the author has analysed and presented the opinions of many others in the field, we read something which begins to sound like his own account of how the mechanics of sacrifice achieved the results. On p. 414 we are brought tantalizingly close to a reasoned account of the causality of atonement:

In all its many variations, redemption had involved some kind of heroic initiative in which the leading protagonist risks his own life, submitting himself entirely to the perils and dangers of the situation, all in order to liberate that which by right belongs to him, but has been brought into bondage by the adversary. It is a willing submission to death in order that the doomed may have life. It is a passion, an agony, a willed acceptance of actual suffering in the faith and conviction that to save others is better than to save oneself.

Eloquent indeed, but on close inspection it offers no deeper explanation than did the writers of the New Testament.

One final quotation from that influential book will make clear that although the drama is described in modern language, the process by which the end result was achieved is still not accounted for. Shortly after the previous quotation, we read on p. 415 the following:

We are convinced that whenever, in limited and imperfect fashion, man submits himself to the pressure, and the onslaught of powers obviously greater than his own, with the object of achieving a fuller freedom, somehow, somewhere this action is of superlative value, even if on the plane of history it ends in apparent disaster. In our own imperfect and limited fashion we are prepared to commit ourselves to this pattern of action as alone worthy of emulation and ultimate praise. What the Christian evangelist has ever been concerned to proclaim is that such an event in space and time received its altogether definitive and final enactment when the Son of God willingly exposed himself to the hosts of evil on Golgotha – cosmic and social, personal and psychological: further that the necessary sequel of Golgotha, expressed in the resurrection event, has opened the gate of everlasting life to those who receive his Spirit and walk in his ways.

Speaking with all due respect to the work of that great scholar, I must confess that I am unable to find in the book anything more explicit than the passages quoted above, which in the last analysis leave the question of cause and effect unanswered rationally.

In 1983 M. Slusser published his article 'Primitive Christian soteriological themes' in the *Journal of Theological Studies*. On p. 555 he makes the important point that in the Arian controversy what was basically at stake was soteriology. In other words the status of the Son of God was not being discussed as a theoretical nicety, but was of crucial importance in the practical matter of his being able to redeem the human race or not. He then goes on to classify the patristic opinions about the liberation, dividing them into five main themes. These he names Victory, Atonement, Revelation, Eschatological Judgement, and Exemplar. Having divided and analysed these themes, he does not offer an answer to the question as to how the process was deemed to have taken place within these five categories.

In 1985 Colin Gunton published an important article in the *Journal of Theological Studies* entitled '*Christus Victor* revisited', in which he reflected, half a century later, on the impact of Gustaf Aulén's epoch-making study *Christus Victor*. I will have more to say about that well-known book in the next chapter. For the present it will suffice to note that Aulén classified the patristic theories of the atonement into three major themes, one of which was that of victory over the devil. He considered that this was the authentic and most widely-held view in patristic times, that it had been overshadowed by St Anselm's theory of satisfaction, and he wrote the book largely to rehabilitate it; hence the title. Not surprisingly Gunton analyses Aulén's use of metaphor in dealing with the conflict between Jesus and evil. (My own use of the word 'conflict' in the previous sentence shows how difficult it is to discuss this matter without recourse to some sort of imagery.) On p. 143 he notes that Aulén had failed to provide rational answers to the main questions; his own words are:

The language of victory enables us to understand how God in Jesus transforms the possibilities for human existence by actively refusing to submit to the forces by which fallen man lives in slavery. Here we return again to a point made by Aulén: 'The deliverance of man from the power of death and the devil is at the same time his deliverance from God's judgement'. The demonized creation operates as the vehicle of judgement by alienation and enslavement. By undergoing these forces himself, God restored human life to himself and so to freedom.

In the last sentence Gunton seems to explain the process by the brief phrase 'by undergoing these forces himself', yet on reflection this is merely a restatement of the happening, and not an explanation.

In 1986 Martin Hengel's important book *The Cross of the Son of God* became available in English translation. He presents an admirable account of the origin of the notion of the redemption in the books of the New Testament, but when it comes to explaining the causality of the actual process, he refrains from going beyond the biblical terminology, as can be seen in a summary statement on the matter:

The death of Jesus on the cross, and his resurrection represent the bearing of human guilt and man's mortal destiny by God himself, who 'identifies' himself with the man Jesus and in so doing overcomes guilt and death for us all. (p. 90)

One would dearly like to know what lies behind the words 'in so doing overcomes guilt', since therein lies the whole mystery of the atonement.

A few years later Gunton published his own book on the subject, *The Actuality of the Atonement* (Edinburgh, 1988). After a careful analysis of the views of other writers, he presents what looks tantalizingly like a reasoned explanation of his own (p. 167): 'Thus representation and substitution are two sides of the one relationship, with Jesus taking our place before God, so that we ourselves may come, reconciled before God.' How that reconciliation was actually brought about he does not say.

My own assessment of Gunton's book received confirmation when it was reviewed by Vernon White in the *Journal of Theological Studies* (1990). On p. 320 he said of Gunton's analysis:

In particular it is still not clear in what sense we should conceive the divine achievement in Jesus as causally constitutive of the present experience of salvation in the Church; nor is it clear in what sense it is constitutive of salvation beyond the bounds of the believing Church, in time and eternity.

In the following year Gunton himself was able to return to the debate (in the *Journal of Theological Studies*) when he reviewed R. Swinburne's book *Responsibility and Atonement* which had appeared that year.

On p. 801 he quoted Swinburne:

The sacrifice of Christ is then Christ giving the most valuable thing he has – his life; both as a lived life of obedience to God, and a laid-down life on the cross – as a present to God, whose benefits flow to others.

Neither the author nor the reviewer says how the benefits flow to others. Later in the review Gunton criticizes Swinburne precisely for that omission:

If the heart of the matter is a gift of great value to God which humans may thereafter plead, what need is there of a death unless it is in some way linked with the ideas of legality and divine judgement? In this book, although the centrality of the death is affirmed, no systematic account of its theological necessity is offered. (p. 804)

The last sentence is of crucial import since it indicates that the cause is still being sought, and that recent writers have not yet given a satisfactory answer to this perennial quest.

The continuing interest aroused by this subject is not confined to the English-speaking world. In 1988 the French theologian Bernard Sesboué published (in Paris) his study entitled *Jésus Christ l'Unique Médiateur*. On p. 321 he comes closest of any sentence in the book to an explanation of the atonement with the eloquent words:

If it was love that led Jesus to the heart of human suffering, his manner of suffering converted the suffering in its turn into love and into the food of love. . . . But it is not the suffering as such which saves us, it is the love with which it is accepted, lived through, and surmounted.

One would not quibble with a single phrase of those statements, but they do not answer the precise question, so urgent for the modern mind, as to how the suffering and the love actually achieved their success in reconciling the human race to God.

The year 1992 saw further publications in this field. T. F. Torrance's book *The Mediation of Christ* was re-issued, and on p. 114 he repeats what has been said so often before, namely that the Bible offers no causal explanation of the workings of sacrifices. To quote his own words: 'No explanation is ever given in the New Testament why atonement for sin involves the blood of sacrifice.'

Then a little further on he puts forward his own explanation: 'The atonement is not to be understood . . . as some external trans-action enacted by Jesus . . . describable in moral or legal terms.' Nothing more explicit than that is offered to the reader.

The last author whose opinion I will cite is John McIntyre, whose book *The Shape of Soteriology* was published in 1992 (Edinburgh). After discussing whether it was necessary for Christ to die, he ends up with the question 'why God could not simply and freely will to forgive our sins' (implying that God could do it without the necessity of the crucifixion). To this question he supplies the following answer:

> Standing as we do on this side of Calvary, we receive a forgiveness which comes to us as an integral whole, forgiveness which is both freely offered to us, and which is costly to God, the two strands . . . woven indissolubly into one. To ask now whether it is possible to have one of these strands at the exclusion of the other is to ask an improper question. (p. 115)

This excursus does not claim to be a summary of every book ever written on the subject, but I trust that it is a fair and representative sample of modern writers in this field. There are two constant characteristics in all of them. Firstly they agree that the Bible gives no explanation of how sacrifices achieved their intended results. When the New Testament authors spoke of the death of Jesus as a sacrifice they were silent about the causality linking his death to human liberation from sin. Secondly the modern authors whom I have quoted remain within the same limits themselves: they do not suggest cogent reasons why Jesus had to suffer, nor how his sufferings achieved reconciliation between God the Father and the human race.

These are the very questions which the modern enquirer, be he agnostic or believer, finds so baffling and for which a reasonable explanation is so urgently needed. It is with this specific quest in mind that I will analyse the various attempts which have been made in the past to account for an otherwise pointlessly cruel death. In this way I intend to prepare the reader for a solution which, I trust, will be deemed satisfactory.

3

⊠ *First attempts at synthesis: the Fathers*

During the first few centuries after the resurrection the scholars of the early Church began to elaborate on the doctrine of the atonement, as they did on all other aspects of the teaching of the New Testament. The background and motivation of this vast intellectual undertaking was, as is well known, their dialogue or disputes with the champions of pagan religions and the philosophers. Somewhat later it also involved controversy with heretics when the orthodox writers were trying to clarify and safeguard the Church's teaching against those who had left the community because they could not accept those doctrines.

The cultural and historical setting which provided the context for the development of patristic thought is so different from that of our own world, that a brief mention of some of the salient differences must be given, in order to keep the doctrinal clarification in a realistic perspective.

In the first place the early Christians were familiar with the phenomenon of sacrifice, and the presuppositions which were accepted by its devotees. In every town and city of the ancient world the temples were present for all to see, and the smoke of sacrifice quite literally rose up to the skies before their eyes every day. The Christians, who were a minority everywhere, knew perfectly well that their neighbours were offering those sacrifices to placate the anger of the gods, and to ask for a variety of benefits for which they felt dependent upon divine good will, whether it was the fertility of the crops, flocks and family, favourable climate, the cessation of epidemics, or success in war. Although the Christians had broken free of that kind of religion, it is worth remembering that their principal area of disagreement with the pagans was not the fact of sacrifices, but the gods to whom they were offered. In the light of Christian revelation their pagan compatriots were seeking favours from non-beings, or perhaps even demons. The practice of sacrifice itself, which had received sanction in the Old Testament from the true God, seems not to have been questioned. The difference between that attitude and that of the modern world needs little comment.

Earlier in this book I pointed out that the New Testament has nothing in common with the pagan religious preoccupation about securing the fruitfulness of nature in farm and family. Instead it is concerned almost exclusively with what we would call personal relationships, in whose context reconciliation with God may legitimately be included. In this respect the modern mind will find no difficulty in appreciating the preoccupations of the New Testament and its commentators in the early centuries. It is a matter of constant interest and anxiety to the contemporary world to be able to enjoy harmonious relationships within the family, and to know how to manage difficult ones in the context of commercial competition, industrial disputes, international rivalries, and even warfare. Since no successful cure has yet been found to the breakdown of these important relationships, in psychoanalysis, sociology, or any other science, religion is still an active contender in the field, claiming a place for moral and spiritual forces in the rightful ordering of human selfishness or altruism and the other influences whose interplay make up the psychological framework in which we develop our lives.

The second major difference between the ancient world and our own which must be borne in mind when studying the atonement is the phenomenon of sin, and the way in which it has been perceived by our remote ancestors and ourselves. It is something of an oversimplification, but basically true, to say that up to a century ago people in Europe generally had a powerful sense of sin. It has almost vanished from the modern scientifically orientated world. Whether our ancestors were always being fair to themselves when they made their self-accusations of sin, is open to question, and lies outside the scope of this book. What is beyond doubt is that they did speak of themselves in that fashion, and presumably were convinced about it. Personally I hold the view that the modern absence of any such sense of sin is not necessarily an advance either in moral progress or psychological maturing. What is really needed is conscientization. This would enable people to perceive moral evil when it really is present, and also to identify its real cause, which may not be within themselves. When properly understood this kind of enquiry would absolve them from the rather lugubrious self-accusations which are to be found in diaries, letters and novels of the nineteenth century, and which now sound so artificial. Let me give one example of a situation where conscientization could have had significant consequences. In the state schools in Germany in the 1930s, a directive was received from the government that Jewish children were to be segregated into separate areas in the classrooms, so that the other children would learn that they were members of a different and inferior race. The implementation of that policy must have required the collaboration of literally thousands of teachers and school administrators. It seems that it was not regarded as a matter of sinfulness. Looking back after the events, one can see just how much morality was at stake. The failure of the Christians to perceive it as a serious moral issue can be accounted for only as an example of the failure in moral training by both Lutheran and Catholic Churches, of which the majority of the population were then members. In modern parlance, what was needed was conscientization to enable the ordinary people to perceive the real moral content of those political decisions, and to appreciate how they must act to oppose them. The passing of the Victorian attitudes of sinfulness, without their being replaced by the process of conscientization, accounts for the modern absence of a sense of sin, and consequently the corresponding lack of a desire for atonement.

Bearing in mind these cultural differences between the ancient world and our own age, we are now in a position to consider what the Fathers wrote about the death of Jesus and the atonement. It will be apparent to the reader in the quotations which follow that many of the Fathers speak of the incarnation itself as the sufficient cause of the redemption, and few of them confine it to the crucifixion. The importance of this observation will become apparent later in the book. I mention it now because since the Middle Ages, in Western Europe, there has been an exclusive concentration on the sufferings of Jesus, which is not consistent with the patristic tradition.

As the teaching of the Fathers on this matter has been treated fully in a number of admirable studies, and since the main conclusions are generally agreed, I will not devote to this exposition more space than is needed for a grasp of the overall position. More detailed exposition and commentary on the patristic material can be found in a variety of readily accessible textbooks.[1]

The first generation of writers, the Apostolic Fathers, did little more than restate the New Testament formulae, adding only a minimum of commentary to make them relevant to the current situation. Ignatius of Antioch is a fair example. He was martyred probably in AD 110, and on his journey to execution in Rome he wrote seven famous letters to the churches in what is now western Turkey. The letter to the community in Smyrna contains a brief statement about the effects of the crucifixion and resurrection. As he wrote he had in mind the views of the Docetists, who maintained that the body of Jesus was not real but an appearance. Consequently for them his birth and death were equally unreal. The implications of this position are alluded to in what Ignatius has to say about the life of Jesus, who was

son of god according to the divine will and power, really born of a virgin and baptized by John that 'all righteousness might be fulfilled' by him, really nailed up in the flesh for us in the time of Pontius Pilate and the tetrarchy of Herod – from this fruit of the tree, that is from his God-blessed passion, we are derived – that he might 'raise up a standard' for all ages through his resurrection, for his saints and faithful people, whether among Jews or gentiles in one body of his Church. For he suffered all this on our account, that we might be saved. And he really suffered, as he really raised himself. Some unbelievers say that he suffered in appearance only. Not so – they themselves are mere apparitions.[2]

The next generation of Christian writers took the matter to a deeper level and elaborated a more detailed theology of the atonement. Of these the best known is Irenaeus. His dates are not absolutely certain, probably AD 130–200. He came from Asia Minor, where as a youth he had heard the preaching of the aged Polycarp, who as a youth had heard St John. It is an interesting indication of the cosmopolitan character of the early Church that he moved eventually to Lyons in the centre of France, where he became their bishop, and where the Christian community spoke Greek. His most important work was written in that language, but it has survived in its entirety only in Latin, and is always referred to by the Latin title *Adversus Haereses*. The heretics in question were the various gnostic groups who taught that there was a series of intermediaries between God the Father and the human race. Irenaeus insisted on the uniqueness of Jesus as the one mediator in conformity with the teaching of the New Testament. This accounts for the way in which he speaks of the life and work of Jesus. The following quotations are from the third book of *Adversus Haereses*:

Christ has brought it about that man is attached and united to God . . . For this it was necessary that the mediator of God and men was of the same nature as the two of them; thus he was able to restore concord between the two, present man to God, and reveal God to men. In practice, how could we have been able to share in the adoption of children, if we had not received from the Son himself communion with the Son, if the Word had not united himself to us, becoming flesh? So he has come, and to all ages, he has rendered to all communion with God.[3]

Irenaeus has always been remembered for his distinctive contribution to the study of the liberation: the concept of recapitulation. The word occurs in the following quotation from Book III of *Adversus Haereses*:

The only begotten Word who is always present with the human race, united and mingled with his handiwork, according to the Father's pleasure, and incarnate, is himself Jesus Christ our Lord, who suffered for us, and rose again for us, and is to come again in the glory of the Father to raise up all flesh to manifest salvation, and apply the rule of just judgement to all who were made by him. Thus there is one God the Father, as we have demonstrated, and one Christ Jesus our Lord who came in fulfilment of God's comprehensive design, and recapitulates all things in himself: he was invisible and became visible; incomprehensible and became comprehensible; impassible and became passible; the Word and made man; recapitulating all things in himself. That as in things above the heavens and in the spiritual and invisible world the Word of God is supreme, so in the visible and physical world he may have pre-eminence, taking to himself the primacy and appointing himself the head of the Church, that he may 'draw all things to himself' in due time.[4]

The key word 'recapitulate' (*anakephalaioō*) has been something of a problem for translators. Usually it is rendered as 'recapitulate', which is literal, but hardly does justice to the Greek by reason of its modern English meaning which has become little more than 'repeat'. The real meaning is much more creative, and denotes something like reassembling the separated limbs of a corpse and bringing them to life again under the control of the head.[5]

Although Irenaeus retains the traditional expressions like 'suffered for us' there is in the above quotation the latent message that the incarnation itself was the principal cause in bringing back union between the human race and the Creator. It would be an overstatement to say that the crucifixion recedes into the background, but it is not presented as the sole sufficient cause of the atonement.

Somewhat later than Irenaeus is the Latin writer Tertullian. He lived in North Africa from roughly 160 to 221, in the thoroughly Latinized culture of the Roman imperial power, in whose army his father had his career. Tertullian himself was trained as a lawyer, and brought the legal concepts with him into theology. He was a prolific writer, and ranks as the father of Latin theology although his time as an orthodox Christian was brief (193–207), in his pilgrimage from paganism via orthodoxy to heresy. It was his training as a lawyer that provided the mass of legalistic concepts which have influenced Latin theology right up to the present day. Quasten has epitomized it thus:

Law permeated his representation of the relation between God and man. God is the giver of law (*De Paen.* I), the judge who administers the law (ibid. II). The gospel is the law of Christians: *Lex proprie nostra, id est evangelium* (*De monog.* 8). Sin is a breach of this law. As such it is *culpa* or *reatus* and offends God (*De Paen.* 3; 5; 7; 10; 11). To do good is to satisfy God (*satisfacere*) (ibid. 5; 6; 7), because God commanded it (*quia Deus praecepit*) (ibid. 4). The fear of God the lawgiver and judge is the beginning of salvation (ibid. 4). *Timor fundamentum salutis est* (*De cultu fem.* 2, 1). God is satisfied by the merit of man (*De Paen.* 2, 6). Here the author uses the term *promereri*. The words debt, satisfaction, guilt, compensation, occur frequently in his writings. He drew the distinction between counsel and precept, between *consilia* and *praecepta dominica*. Whereas Irenaeus conceived salvation as a divine economy (*Adv. Haer.* III, 24, 1), Tertullian speaks of *salutaris disciplina* (*De Pat.* 12), a discipline ordained of God through Christ.[6]

In view of this legalistic approach to the whole of theology it is not surprising that his treatment of sin and forgiveness was presented in predominantly legal concepts. What is more surprising is that its influence on later Latin theology was so powerful.

For the purposes of the present book the concept of satisfaction is the most important. It dominated his understanding of reconciliation. By this he meant that moral badness required some form of compensation if it were to be put right. He applied this concept to the treatment of individual sin and its forgiveness, and not to the wider context of Christ's atoning for the sins of all humanity. This precision is important, because the fact is often overlooked. Nevertheless it was inevitable that as the concept of satisfaction had been introduced into the understanding of the reconciliation of individual sinners, it would only be a matter of time until someone applied it to the wider field of reconciling the world to God. Indeed the idea is not far below the surface, as will be seen in the next quotation. It is taken from his *De Fuga in Persecutione*, and the immediate context is quite literally about purchasing immunity from prosecution in times of persecution:

To ransom with money a man whom Christ redeemed with his own blood, is not this unworthy of God and his ways of dealing with man? For he spared not his own son . . . 'he was led as a sheep to the slaughter' . . . and delivered up to death on a cross. 'And all this that he might win us away from our sins.' The sun made over the day of our purchase, our release was effected in the underworld, our contract made in heaven; the eternal gates were raised up, that the king of glory might enter, who has bought man from earth, nay from the underworld, to set him in heaven. What kind of man is he who strives against Christ, nay, who depreciates and soils the merchandise which he acquired at so great a price, the price of his most precious blood? Why, it were better to flee than to be reduced in price, for that is what happens if a man puts on himself a lesser value than did Christ. And the Lord ransomed him from the angelic powers who rule the world, from the spirits of iniquity, from the darkness of this world, from eternal judgement, from everlasting death: while you are bargaining for him with an informer, or soldier, or some petty official on the sly, as if you were passing stolen goods.[7]

Clearly Tertullian has taken the intellectual explanation of the atonement further than the restatement of the New Testament formulae. His observations do not amount to a fully worked-out explanation of the cause and effect of the work of Christ. The frequency with which he uses terms like purchase and ransom is an indication of the path which Latin theology would take later on. The orientation towards a forensic theory of redemption had already been set, and its implications would be worked out to their logical conclusion by the Western medieval scholars.

At the opposite end of the Mediterranean Tertullian's latter years coincided with the flowering in Egypt of the genius Origen (186–254). In spite of the latter's extensive travels the two men never met nor corresponded. For the details of the life and work of this unconventional scholar, I must refer the reader to the standard textbooks of patrology. For my present purposes it will suffice to point out that his massive literary output was concerned mainly with the Scriptures, establishing the reliability of the texts, and commenting on them. Nevertheless the intellectual climate of that time did not admit of total specialization, and in his polemical treatises he had ample opportunity to expound many particular points of Christian theology, including the atonement. His original contribution to the study of this field was his application to the death of Christ of the concept of propitiation. The sheer volume of his writings is so vast that it is difficult to select the most apposite expositions of the theology of the atonement, nevertheless the following passage from his commentary on the Book of Numbers shows clearly how he thought about the matter:

It may well be that as our Lord and Saviour . . . bestowed remission of sins on the whole world, so also the blood of others, holy and righteous men . . . has been shed for the expiation, in some part of the people . . . Christ is spoken of as a lamb because his willingness and goodness, by which he made God again propitious to men and bestowed pardon for sins, stood for the human race as a lamb, a spotless and innocent victim, a victim by which heaven is believed to be reconciled to men . . . While there are sins there must needs be required sacrificial victims for sins. For suppose for argument's sake that there had been no sin. Had there been no sin the Son of God would not have been constrained to become a lamb, nor would there have been need for him to be incarnate and to be put to death; but he would have remained what he was in the beginning, God the word; but since sin entered into the world, and sin of necessity required propitiation, and propitiation cannot be effected save by a sacrificial victim, such a victim had to be provided for sin. And inasmuch as there were different and various kinds of sin, sacrifices of diverse animals were enjoined, to fit the various types of sin . . . Besides things on earth, things in heaven also stand in need of propitiation. For the heavens are threatened with destruction: as the prophet says, 'The heavens will perish; and they shall grow old, like a garment, and thou shalt fold them up like a robe, and they will be changed'. Think therefore of the purification of the whole universe, the things in heaven, things on earth, and things beneath the earth: what great numbers of victims all these would need! What bullocks, lambs, and goats! But for all these there is one Lamb, who could 'take away the sin of the whole world'. Therefore the other victims ceased.[8]

In spite of his copious exposition, it is instructive for the modern reader to note how much Origen takes for granted. In the passage cited above, he states without comment as if it is self-evident that 'while there are sins there must needs be required sacrificial victims for sins', and further on, 'sin of necessity required propitiation, and propitiation cannot be effected save by a sacrificial victim'. It is precisely those unquestioned assumptions that the modern mind finds baffling and for which we feel the need of convincing explanations. As I pointed out at the beginning of this chapter, the early Christians accepted the presuppositions about sacrifices which were shared by their pagan contemporaries and the Jews, both of their own time and of antiquity. The Christians were wrestling with the theological problems entailed in the uniqueness and incomparable efficacy of the one sacrifice of Christ.

Roughly a century after Origen the Church went through two quantum leaps in its historical development, namely the Arian controversy and the official toleration of Christianity by Constantine. Both factors had far-reaching results which were scarcely foreseeable by the people who lived through them. The Arian dispute was not wholly sterile in its results, and the Constantinian Edict of Toleration was not totally beneficial.

For the purposes of this present study, it is sufficient to point out that in controversy with the Arians the orthodox Christians were compelled to clarify the status of the Son of God, which is not unambiguously clear in the New Testament. They were not concerned primarily with his work of liberation from sin, but with his status in relation to God the Father. Nevertheless it was not an academic dispute, and just below the surface lay the practical issue of the efficacy of the atonement. If he were not divine, he could not have redeemed the whole human race, since the magnitude of such a task was clearly beyond the capabilities of any created (and therefore limited) being. This may account for the bitterness and passion which was engendered in the ferocious quarrels between the Orthodox and the Arians. They realized that what was at stake was vital to human destiny; it was not an academic dispute for its own sake.

Bearing in mind these priorities we can appreciate why the definition of Nicaea (AD 325) focuses explicitly on the Son's equality with the Father, and mentions atonement indirectly. The Creed indicates that the motive for the incarnation was 'for us and for our salvation', and then goes on to speak briefly of the birth, death and resurrection of Jesus, saying merely that he was crucified 'for us'. As is well known, it had been the intention of the bishops at the Council to declare that the Son was divine and equal to the Father (being of the same nature). The incarnation, and the relationship between the divine and the human in Jesus, was not then a matter of dispute; so it was stated factually without elaboration. The atonement was still less a matter of disagreement, and was alluded to only by implication in the brief phrases about the motive of the incarnation and crucifixion. In other words, the

Council of Nicaea left open the whole question as to how the atonement was effected, and placed therefore no limits on the directions which speculative theory might subsequently embark upon in the quest for a rational solution to this problem. Later Councils did not alter the position. The fact of the atonement has never been disputed among Christians to a degree which would warrant the intervention of the teaching authority. To this day the precise causal process has remained an open question among theologians.

Unfortunately the Council did not put an end to the Arian heresy; if anything, the years which followed showed an increase in the amplitude, the bitterness, and the political interventions in the controversy.

The champion of orthodoxy was Athanasius, the bishop of Alexandria. Not long after the Council he was hounded out of his diocese and spent most of the remainder of his life on the move or in hiding. It is astounding that he was able to combine this pattern of life with a vigorous literary output. It was in this period of post-conciliar disputes that he composed what was perhaps the most important patristic treatise on the redemption, namely *The Incarnation of the Word*, completed probably in 336.[9] In that work he dealt with the incarnation in the context of the Arian denial that the Son was equal to the Father. Basically the same preoccupations were in his mind when he wrote the three *Orationes contra Arianos*. The dating of these three has been a matter of considerable debate and dates as far apart as 338 and 362 have had their supporters; it lies outside the scope of this book to follow further the disputes about the dating. What is relevant is to bear in mind that Athanasius had perceived that the efficacity of the atonement was at stake in the quarrel with the Arians. It was not a quasi-philosophical debate conducted within the categories of Greek philosophy, but an intensely practical matter. Nevertheless, granted the intellectual climate of the time, it was inevitable that it would be conducted in the terms derived from Greek philosophy. The basic insight of Athanasius, which will be seen in the following quotations, was that if the Son of God had not been divine, he could not have saved the human race from sin and its consequences. This intensely practical aspect of the dispute may well explain how the controversy was taken up and followed with enthusiasm, among monks and bishops (understandably), and, less predictably, by politicians and the sailors on the ships in harbour in Alexandria.

My first quotation is from the second *Oratio adversus Arianos*, chapters 59 and 60:

If the Son was a creature, mankind would be as mortal as before, because it would not have been united to God. In reality a creature cannot unite other creatures to God: the creature in question has need also of someone who can effect the union. One part of creation cannot give salvation to creation, because it too needs it. So God sent his own son. He having taken up created flesh has become the son of man. Now, all men had been condemned to death. But he who is innocent has offered for all his body to death, with the result that all have died because of him, and all are dead in him, and the sentence which condemned us is accomplished. But further, by him we are all delivered from sin and from the curse, we are raised up from the dead, and clothed with immortality and incorruptibility, we will dwell in eternity.[10]

The same theological outlook is to be seen in the next quotation, from *The Incarnation of the Word*, chapter 9:

The Word, perceiving that not otherwise could the corruption of men be undone, save by death as a necessary condition, while it was impossible for the Word to suffer death, being immortal, and the Son of the Father; to this end he takes to himself a body capable of death, that it by partaking of the Word who is above all, might be worthy to die instead of all, and might because of the Word which was come to dwell in it remain incorruptible, and that henceforth corruption might be stayed from all by the grace of the resurrection. Whence by offering unto death the body He himself had taken, as an offering and sacrifice free from any stain, straightaway He put away death from all his peers by the offering of an equivalent. For being over all, the Word of God naturally by offering his own temple and corporeal instrument for the life of all satisfied the debt by his death. And thus He, the incorruptible Son of God, being conjoined with all by a like nature, naturally clothed all with incorruption by promise of the resurrection. For the actual corruption in death has no longer holding-ground against men, by reason of the Word, which by his own body has come to dwell among them.[11]

For the modern reader Athanasius' presuppositions are tantalizing. In the above quotation he states without comment that 'not otherwise could the corruption of men be undone, save by death as a necessary condition'. Clearly his readers understood it as a self-evident principle, but it is the kind of axiom which the modern mind cannot accept, and for which a reasoned explanation must be provided.

While the Arian controversy was being pursued for more than half a century, with increasing bitterness, the Church was acquiring more privileges and freedom during the reign of Constantine. This freedom, and even more so the privileges, were to have unforeseeable consequences in the future. Of immediate concern here is the fact that with the cessation of persecution conditions were created in which theology could flourish. Vast numbers of large churches were built, the liturgy became more elaborate, and preaching (which consisted of homilies on the whole of the Scriptures) provided preachers with an opportunity to explain every aspect of God's dealings with the human race. Scholars had the time, and mostly the tranquillity, in which to clarify and express their ideas, and exchange them with like-minded souls thanks to the ease with which books, letters, and homilies could be circulated. This interchange of ideas was assisted to no small extent by the comparative peace of the empire, its excellent system of roads and communications, and also by the increasing activity of translators. A glance at any textbook of patrology will indicate the veritable explosion of intellectual activity which took place from the middle of the fourth century. Disputes with pagans and heretics, both of which categories of debate took place within the framework of Hellenic culture, provided the stimuli for Christian theology to develop its first magnificent flowering. Such was the background of the next generation of patristic writers, whose opinions about the atonement must now be studied. I will present this exposition quite briefly because, as I have said earlier, the matter has been researched thoroughly and can be read in more detail in many standard textbooks and specialized studies.

Perhaps the most famous group of the Fathers of this period is the trio known, from their birthplace in central Turkey, as the Cappadocian Fathers. The oldest is St Basil, who was born about 330. He wrote no formal treatise on the atonement, but his considerations on the matter can be seen clearly from references to it in other contexts. For example in his *Homily on Psalm 48* he says the following:

Every human soul has submitted to the evil yoke of slavery; slavery to the common enemy of all: mankind has been despoiled of the liberty which was the gift of the creator and has been brought into captivity through sin. Now, for any captive to recover his liberty, a ransom is required: nor is it possible for a brother to ransom his brother, nor for each to ransom himself; for the ransomer must be far superior to the conquered slave. Man is utterly powerless to make atonement to God for the sinner, since every man is charged with sin . . . Therefore do not seek a brother to effect your ransom. But there is one superior to our nature; not a mere man, but one who is man and God, Jesus Christ, who alone is able to make atonement for us all, because 'God appointed him as the expiation, through faith, by his blood'. What can man find of such value that he may give it for the ransoming of his Son? One thing has been found of such worth as to pay the price for all mankind: the holy and most precious blood of our Lord Jesus Christ, which he poured out on our behalf and for us all.[12]

His message is relatively simple and his presuppositions are equally clear. Concepts like ransom are taken from the Scriptures and from the customs of his age. His manner of writing about ransom and its consequences makes it clear that his hearers and readers would not have had any difficulty in comprehending the underlying principles which he does not trouble to explain.

Basil's lifelong friend since their student days in Athens was the slightly younger St Gregory Nazianzen (332–390). His background and cultural formation were the same as Basil's; so too were his theological preoccupations. The Cappadocians, like all orthodox writers of that period, were busy clarifying the divinity of the Son of God, and working out the implications of that doctrine. Like Basil he did not write a specific treatise on the atonement, but clearly he reflected upon it. One interesting passage in which he discusses it raises some important questions about the 'ransom' principle which he leaves (tantalizingly) unanswered:

We have now to examine a point of doctrine which has generally been overlooked, though to me it seems to deserve careful enquiry. The question is: To whom was offered the blood that was shed for us, and why was it offered, this precious and glorious blood of our God, our high priest, our sacrifice? We were held captive by the Evil One, for we had been 'sold into the bondage of sin', and our wickedness was the price we paid for our pleasure. Now a ransom is normally paid only to the captor; and so the question is: To whom was this ransom offered, and why? To the Evil One? What an outrage! If it is supposed not merely that the thief received a ransom from God, but that the ransom is God himself – a payment for his act of arbitrary power so excessive that it certainly justified his releasing us! If it was paid to the Father, I ask first why? We were not held captive by him. Secondly what reason can be given why the blood of the only-begotten should be pleasing to the Father? For he did not accept even Isaac when he was offered by his father, but gave a substitute for the sacrifice, a lamb to take the place of the rational victim. Is it not clear that the Father accepts the sacrifice not because he demanded it, but because this was part of the divine plan, since man had to be sanctified by the humanity of God: so that he might rescue us by overcoming the tyrant by force, and bring us back to himself through the mediation of the Son, who carried out this divine plan to the honour of the Father, to whom he clearly delivers up all things? We have said just so much about Christ. There are many more things which must be passed over in reverent silence.[13]

The passage just quoted is frustrating, since Gregory raises some of the questions which are perplexing to the modern mind, but scarcely supplies a satisfactory answer. In stating that the Father accepted the sacrifice, not because he needed it, but because it was part of the divine plan, he came very close to the view of Aquinas (to be discussed further on) that the sacrifice was fitting, but not absolutely necessary. In the same sentence he seems to indicate that the atonement was effected basically by the incarnation itself, rather than by any particular activity of Christ during his earthly life. This is a view which is to be seen elsewhere among the Fathers. In spite of asking these penetrating questions, he does not break out completely from the limitations of the imagery in which the whole matter was then discussed and understood, as can be seen by the phrase 'that he might rescue us by overcoming the tyrant by force'. Once again as with so many of the ancient writers, the modern reader is left with no answers to the precise questions which so much exercise our minds as we reflect upon the necessity or purpose of the crucifixion.

The third member of the famous Cappadocian trio was the younger brother of St Basil, St Gregory of Nyssa (*c.* 335–394). He has the distinction of being the writer who most clearly presents the atonement as flowing directly from the incarnation, with the result that the crucifixion is relegated to a comparatively minor place. I will quote from his writings more fully because it is important to emphasize this aspect of the liberating work of Christ, in view of the almost exclusive concentration on the crucifixion from the period of the late Middle Ages.

Commenting upon the words of Jesus to Mary Magdalene 'Touch me not' (John 20:17) he says:

Our life had been alienated from God; and its return to the high and heavenly place was beyond its own unaided contrivance. For this reason as the Apostle says, 'he who had no acquaintance with sin is made to be sin' and frees us from the curse by making our curse his own; and taking up the enmity which had come between us and God 'he slew (in the words of the Apostle) the enmity in his own person'. Sin indeed was the enmity. Thus by becoming what we were, through his own person he again united humanity to God. For through purity he brought into the closest kinship with the Father of our nature that 'new man which is created after the likeness of God, in whom the whole fullness of the godhead dwelt in bodily form', and along with himself he drew to the same state of grace all the nature which shares in his human body and is akin to him.[14]

It is difficult to overstate the significance of the sentence in the above passage where he states that 'by becoming what we were, through his own person he again united humanity to God'. It would seem that nothing further was required for the atonement above and beyond the incarnation. Elsewhere, though, Gregory uses the familiar image of ransom, but, somewhat surprisingly for the modern reader, the payment of the ransom is effected by the fact that the Son of God enters the human race, as it were leaving heaven and going into prison. This preliminary observation is necessary to make sense of a somewhat obscure passage about the need to deceive the devil:

For you have a demonstration of goodness, wisdom, and justice in the device by which the divine power became accessible through investment in a human body so that the divine plan for us should not be thwarted by the fear inspired by a manifestation of the divinity. His choosing to save man is evidence of his goodness; his making the ransoming of the captive a matter of exchange displays his justice; while his pre-eminent wisdom is demonstrated by the device by which something was made accessible to the enemy which had been beyond his grasp. In order that the exchange for us might be easily accepted by him who sought for it the divine nature was concealed under the veil of our human nature so that as with a greedy fish, the hook of divinity might be swallowed along with the bait of the flesh.[15]

The crucifixion is definitely in the background and not a major feature in Gregory's understanding of the atonement. In one passage he speaks of it as if it were little more than the completion of the incarnation, namely that Christ could not have been adequately human unless he had experienced that which is unavoidable for all men, namely death:

Yet it may be that one who had a thorough and exact understanding of the revelation would say with more justification that the birth was accepted for the sake of the death rather than that the death followed as a necessary consequence of the birth. For he who exists eternally did not submit to a bodily birth because he wanted to live, but in order to recall us from death to life. Then since what was needed was the ascent of the whole of our nature from death to renewal of life, he stretched out a hand as it were over the prostrate body, and in bending down to our dead corpse he came so near to death as to come into contact with our state of mortality and by his own body to bestow on human nature a beginning of the resurrection, by raising up through his power the whole of man along with himself. For that humanity which received the godhead and through the resurrection was raised up with the godhead, came from no other source than from the mass of human nature. Therefore just as in our human body the activity of one of the sense organs communicates a sensation which is felt in common by the whole system which is united with that particular member; so the resurrection of a member passes to the whole race, as though the whole of humanity were one living being; and it is distributed from the part to the whole, by reason of the continuity and solidarity of the human race.[16]

Once again the principal link of causality is depicted as the incarnation itself, leading on to the general resurrection. The death of Jesus is anything but prominent in these perspectives.

Not far from the last quotation and in the same section of the *Oratio Catechetica*, Gregory presents the crucifixion in purely symbolic terms, as follows:

This is what we learn from the cross. It is divided into four parts, so that there are four projections from the centre, where the whole figure converges. This teaches us that he who was stretched out at the destined hour, when by his death he fulfilled the redemptive plan, is he who binds together all things in himself, bringing together in harmonious and concordant unity the diverse natures of existing things. For in all that exists there is the conception of something above, or below, or else thought passes to the boundaries on either side. Thus if you consider the system of things above the heavens, or beneath the earth, or the boundaries of the universe on either side, everywhere your thought is preceded and met by deity, which alone is observed in all that exists in every part and holds all things together in existence . . . The great Paul starts from the spectacle of the cross when he initiates the people of Ephesus, and instils in them the power through his teaching to know what is the depth and height and breadth and length. For he names each projection of the cross by its proper appellation: the upper part he calls 'the height' and the lower 'the depth', the extensions on either side 'the breadth and the length'.[17]

Much of what he says is unfamiliar, and perhaps unhelpful to the modern reader, but it is instructive to reflect upon the wide scope of his soteriology. Basically it was the incarnation itself which achieved the reuniting of the human race with God, from whom we had become estranged through sin. The crucifixion and the resurrection have their places in this large-scale plan, but they are of secondary importance in comparison with the incarnation itself. I feel that it is worth stressing this point, because the doctrine has been distorted in recent years by an almost exclusive connection between the crucifixion and the atonement.

A somewhat different intellectual perspective is to be found in St John Chrysostom (*c.* 350–407). He came from Antioch, where he had been formed in the tradition of more literal interpretation of the Scriptures than was to be found in Alexandria, the other great centre of theology. Towards the end of his life he became, reluctantly, the bishop of Constantinople, and he died in circumstances which make him one of the most heroic and tragic of the Church's scholars. He was expelled from the bishopric of Constantinople by the hostility and jealousy of his political enemies, and died of hardships in exile. He is principally renowned for his comprehensive commentaries on many books of the Bible, in the course of which he was presented with the opportunity of explaining the atonement.

In his commentary on the fourth gospel he examines the passage (John 12:31) where Jesus says 'Now is the judgement of this world: now the prince of this world will be cast out'. He expands the scriptural text by expanding it to a soliloquy which he places on the lips of Jesus.

It is as if he said, 'There will be a trial and justice will be done . . . Why then did he assail me and hand me over to death? Why did he put into the soul of Judas the resolve to bring about my death?'

Then Chrysostom continues:

Do not tell me now that God had so ordained it; for the fulfilment of God's plan does not belong to the devil, but to God's own wisdom; let us observe the treatment of the evil one. How then is 'the world to be judged in me'? It is as if the devil was being examined before a court in session. Very well. You put them all to death because you found them guilty of sin: but why did you put the Christ to death? Is it not obvious that you acted unjustly? Therefore all the world shall be acquitted through him.[18]

As with many of the patristic writings the modern reader would dearly like to ask further: how exactly was the world acquitted? It is stated by Chrysostom as if it were obvious, but the modern reader does not find it so.

The last great representative of the school of Alexandria was St Cyril, who succeeded to the episcopal throne on the death of his uncle Theophilus in 412. The date of his birth is not known, but his death occurred in 444, after years of turbulent controversy with the Nestorians. His commentary on the gospel of St John, which was composed before the Nestorian crisis, provided the occasion for him to expound his understanding of the redemption.

The first extract which I will cite describes the salvific process as if it is a straightforward consequence of the incarnation. Nothing is said about the crucifixion. However the second extract from the commentary on St John supplies the complementary evaluation of the role of the sufferings of Christ.

Commenting on chapter 11, he says:

> He was in one and the same being, God and man. Thus he united in himself two natures, widely separated in themselves, and he effected man's sharing and participation in the divine nature. In reality, the communication of the Holy Spirit has come down to us; the Spirit has dwelt in us too. This took its beginning in Christ, and was realized first of all in him. When in reality he became like us, that is to say man, he was anointed and consecrated. Although in his divine nature insofar as he came from the Father, he himself sanctified by his own Spirit the temple of his flesh, and also all the universe which he had created, in the measure that all needed sanctification. The mystery which took place in Christ is thus the beginning and the means of our sharing in the Spirit and of our union with God.[19]

In his exposition of chapter 12 of St John he speaks of the passion of Christ:

> He was scourged unjustly to deliver us from well deserved penalties; he received blows and lashes in order that we might resist Satan and avoid the sin aggravated by prevarication. We are saying in effect, and it is a fully orthodox sentiment, that all the sufferings of Christ came about on account of us and for our sake, and that they have the power to remove and destroy the evils which come upon us, justly, because of sin.[20]

As with so many of the Fathers, Cyril does not explain how the sufferings of Christ brought about mankind's deliverance from sin and its consequences. It seems that he almost took this for granted in the understanding of his hearers, and that he spelt out in far greater detail in almost automatic sanctification of the human race as a direct result of the incarnation.

Turning once again to the Latin writers, I will pass over a number of them and move straight away to St Augustine. He outshone all his predecessors in the West, and exercised an unequalled influence on the subsequent development of theology in Europe. This was due to the great volume of his literary output, covering practically every area of theology, but more especially it was due to his sheer brilliance as an original thinker. In his numerous books, sermons and letters he alluded frequently to the atonement, and I will offer a few quotations which are representative but by no means exhaustive.

In his treatise on the Trinity, written about 410–416, Augustine asks himself some penetrating questions about the death of Jesus. In the context of Romans 5:9 he says:

But what is the meaning of 'made righteous in his blood'? What power is there in this blood, I demand, that believers are made righteous in it? And what of 'reconciled through the death of his Son'? Is it really the case that when God the Father was angry with us, he saw the death of his Son for us, and was appeased? Are we to suppose that his Son was appeased, so much that he deigned even to die for us: while the Father remained so angry that he would not be appeased unless his Son died for us? What of that other passage by the Teacher of the Nations: what are we to say in the face of this? 'If God is on our side, who is against us? God did not grudge his own Son but gave him up for us all: with this gift can he fail to bestow all his gifts on us?' Can we suppose that the Father would have given his own Son for us, ungrudgingly, had he not already been appeased? Is there not a contradiction here? The one passage says that the Son died and the Father was reconciled to us by his death: the other speaks as if the Father loved us before, and himself gave his Son . . . Nor was the Son given up as if against his will, since it has been said of him, 'He loved me and gave himself up for me'. Everything is the combined work of the Father, the Son and the Spirit of both, in equal and harmonious activity: yet 'we have been made righteous in Christ's blood' and 'reconciled to God through the death of his Son'. How this can be I will do my best to explain sufficiently for our present purpose.

By a kind of divine justice the human race was handed over to the devil's power, since the sin of the first man passed at birth to all who were born by the intercourse of the two sexes and the debt of the first parents bound all their posterity . . . The method by which man was surrendered to the devil's power ought not to be understood in the sense that it was God's act, or the result of God's command: rather he merely permitted it, but he did so with justice. When God deserted the sinner the instigator of sin rushed in. Yet God did not so desert his creatures as not to show himself to him as God the creator and life giver, and provider, even amid the ills of punishment, of many good things for evil mankind. In his wrath he did not withhold his mercies. Nor did he let man go from the reach of his power, when he allowed him to pass into the power of the devil; not even the devil himself is removed from the power of the Omnipotent, nor from his goodness. Whence could even the malignant angels derive existence except through him who is the source of all life? Thus the commission of sins subjected man to the devil through the just anger of God; while the remission of sin, through the generous reconciliation of God, rescued man from the devil.

However the devil had to be overcome not by God's power, but by his justice. What is more powerful than the Omnipotent? What creature's power can be compared with the creator's? But the devil, warped by his own perversity, fell in love with power, and abandoned justice and attacked it; for men also imitate the devil in this way, in so far as they neglect and even hate justice and aim at power, gloating in its acquisition or inflamed with lust for it. Therefore God decided that to rescue man from the devil's power the devil should be overcome by justice not by power: not because power is to be eschewed as something evil; but the right order must be kept, and justice has precedence.

And what is the justice by which the devil has been conquered? Surely it is the justice of Christ. And how has he been conquered? Because the devil put Christ to death, although he found in him nothing that deserved death. And it is surely just that the debtors he held should be set free when they believe in him whom he put to death when no debt was owing . . . [21]

It is interesting to observe that the forensic orientation first set by Tertullian is pursued so thoroughly by Augustine. Although it is a clearly reasoned line of argument on the basis of the imagery of debts and justice, for the modern reader it raises as many questions as it answers. Quite apart from the personification of the devils, what is one to make of the concept of justice operating between such unequal persons as God, the devils (whom Augustine envisages basically as angels), and humans? Important precisions would be introduced by Anselm, about whom I will speak in the next chapter, but for the moment it is sufficient to note that there is much in the above passage that the modern reader would find totally unhelpful in trying to come to terms with the image of an angry God requiring a brutal death for his Son.

When he chose, St Augustine could be very succinct, as can be seen from the next quotation from the same treatise on the Trinity:

By his death, the one most real sacrifice offered for us, he purged, abolished, and extinguished whatever guilt there was which gave just ground for the principalities and powers to hold us in custody for our punishment.[22]

I will conclude this survey of patristic opinion with St Gregory the Great, in whom we see the continuation of the forensic approach initiated by Tertullian. In his *Moralia* he introduces the concept of merit into the redemptive work of Christ.

The only Son of the Father has come among us: from us he has taken human nature without committing any fault. He had to be in effect without sin, he being the one who would intervene for the sinners . . . in so intervening for sinners, he has shown himself to be the just one, able to merit the pardon for the others.[23]

This legalistic approach to the atonement was destined to be the principal orientation of Western thinking for centuries to come. It can be seen in the liturgy as well as in popular prayers; it occurs also in the medieval mystery plays, in the carols, and in the religious art of that period. Indeed, as the Middle Ages drew to a close, the paintings, particularly of the Flemish and Rhineland schools, display a virtual obsession with the physical sufferings of Christ. Practically nothing else was considered in the work of redemption except the bodily injuries and death of Jesus. For example, it is not without significance that the well-known devotion, the Stations of the Cross, finishes with Jesus in the tomb at the final station. One wonders why they did not have the resurrection as the concluding picture. To this day the Catholic churches of the West have the crucifix as their principal symbol, whereas the Orthodox churches in the East display the *Christos Pantokratōr* (the icon of the resurrection) in the apses of their churches. Basically it is all traceable to the overemphasis on the legalistic understanding of the atonement by the Latin Fathers.

At the end of this brief survey of patristic opinions on the process of human liberation, a number of conclusions can be drawn.

First of all, the Fathers confined themselves to explanations of the scriptural text in a rather descriptive fashion, expanding what the New Testament writers had said, rather than analysing them in depth. We do not see here the kind of profound philosophical investigation and elaboration which they brought to bear on the doctrines of the Trinity and the incarnation. Basically it was because there were no great disputes about the atonement, unlike the profound controversies which raged over the other two doctrines.

Secondly, it is most important to note that within the limitations of their explanations of the atonement they are not confined to any one line of thought. The incarnation is presented by some of them as the cause of the redemption, just as strongly as the crucifixion. The latter is explained variously as a victory over the devil, or the payment of a debt, or indeed a ransom. I wish to stress this diversity because it will be important later in applying a corrective to the excessive reliance on the crucifixion as the sole cause of the atonement in later Western theology.

So whereas the Fathers are agreed that Christ has saved the human race from sin and its consequences, there was no unanimous tradition as to how this momentous achievement was brought about. In view of the importance which Catholic theology attaches to Tradition (with a capital T), and since the agreement of the Fathers is a normative criterion in the establishment of this source of doctrine, it is equally important in the doctrine of the atonement to realize that consensus is absent as to how the atonement was brought about. It is instructive to cite a couple of standard authors on the matter. In the most comprehensive modern history of dogma, B. Studer (the author of the section on soteriology) has this to say of the matter:

The Church in patristic times did not explicitly and in dogmatic fashion determine how the salvific process was to be understood . . . Jesus Christ could only redeem us since he was truly God and truly man.[24]

Better known to English speakers is the work of J. N. D. Kelly, whose assessment is much the same:

Indeed while the conviction of redemption through Christ has always been the motive force of christian faith, no final and universally accepted definition of the manner of its achievement has been formulated to this day.[25]

NOTES

1 G. Aulén, *Christus Victor* (London, 1953); H. E. W. Turner, *The Patristic Doctrine of the Redemption* (London, 1952); F. W. Dillistone, *The Christian Understanding of the Atonement* (London, 1968); J. N. D. Kelly, *Early Christian Doctrines* (5th edition; London, 1976); B. Studer in *Handbuch der Dogmengeschichte* , vol. III, 2a (Freiburg, 1978).

2 Ignatius, *Letter to the Church at Smyrna*, I and II: Migne, *Patrologia Graeca* (hereafter referred to as PG) 5, 707–708. The English translations in this chapter are either my own, or taken from standard reference works such as *Ancient Christian Writers*, ed. J. Kleist (London, 1946); *Library of the Nicene and Post-Nicene Fathers* (Grand Rapids, Michigan, 1952); H. Bettenson, *The Early Christian Fathers* and *The Later Christian Fathers* (Oxford, 1969 and 1974).

3 Irenaeus, *Adversus Haereses*, III, 18, 7: PG 7, 937.

4 *Adversus Haereses*, III, 16, 6: PG 7, 925.

5 W. Bauer, *Greek–English Lexicon of the New Testament and Other Early Christian Literature* (Chicago and London, 1979), p. 54; G. Lampe, *Patristic Greek Lexicon* (Oxford, 1961), p. 106.

6 J. Quasten, *Patrology* (Westminster, Maryland, 1960), vol. 2, p. 322.

7 Tertullian, *De Fuga in Persecutione*, XII: Migne, *Patrologia Latina* (hereafter PL) 2, 135.

8 Origen, *Homily on Numbers*, XXIV, 1; PG 13, 755.

9 Quasten, op. cit., vol. 3, p. 24, following E. Schwartz.

10 Athanasius, *II Contra Arianos*, 59 and 60: PG 26, 293–296.

11 Athanasius, *The Incarnation of the Word*, IX, in the translation of *Library of Nicene and Post-Nicene Fathers*.

12 Basil of Caesarea, *Homily on Psalm 48:3*: PG 29, 437–438.

13 Gregory Nazianzen, *Oratio XLV*, 22: PG 36, 653–654.

14 Gregory of Nyssa, *Contra Eunomium*, XII: PG 45, 897–898.

15 Gregory of Nyssa, *Oratio Catechetica* XXI–XXIV: PG 45, 57–64.

16 *Oratio Catechetica* XXXII: PG 45, 77–78.

17 Ibid.

18 John Chrysostom, *Homily 67 on John*, XII: PG 59, 311–312.

19 Cyril of Alexandria, *Commentary on John*, XI:11: PG 74, 557.

20 *Commentary on John*, XII: PG 74, 628.

21 Augustine, *De Trinitate*, XIII, 13, 15 and 16: PL 42, 1026–1030.

22 *De Trinitate*, IV, 17: PL 42, 902.

23 Gregory the Great, *Moralia*, XXIV, 2, 4: PL 76, 289.

24 Studer, op. cit., vol. III, 2a, pp. 224, 225. The latter judgement is supported also by Quasten, op. cit., vol. 3, p. 8.

25 Kelly, op. cit., p. 163.

4

⊠ *Medieval solutions to the problems*

After the patristic age, the second great flowering of theology took place in the twelfth and thirteenth centuries. The cultural factors which produced this renaissance were somewhat different from those which stimulated the Fathers. The socio-economic background was the reasonably peaceful, stable and wealthy feudal society of Western Europe at that time. The dynamic forces were the rediscovery of Greek philosophy and Roman law, whose fertile conjunction with traditional Christian theology resulted in a remarkable creative period of intellectual development. At that time the Church was not troubled by any major heresy, and the characteristic literary products of the period were the massive systematic compilations of the whole of what is now called dogmatic, moral, and spiritual theology.

I do not intend to repeat the information about this intellectual movement, which is to be found in countless reference books, except to mention one factor which is frequently overlooked, namely that it was not simply the meeting of ideas which generated this theological renaissance; progress was also facilitated at the institutional level. It was at this time that universities emerged as something almost entirely new. They were different from the cathedral schools which had preceded them, in that they received their charters from the Popes. This had two important consequences. They awarded degrees which were valid throughout Christendom, and more importantly they were under the immediate jurisdiction of the papacy and therefore exempt from that of the local bishops. It goes without saying that they were also outside the jurisdiction of the local kings, since they were ecclesiastical institutions. As a result of this double exemption they enjoyed greater freedom than any other medieval institutions. This system of juridical independence or control may seem light-years away from modern perspectives, but in one respect it was unexpectedly familiar. It has been argued that this legal freedom was the basis of the academic freedom which is taken for granted in universities today.

The teachers and students of those early universities moved about Europe with remarkable ease, speaking and writing in the same language (Latin) and sharing the same intellectual background whether in Oxford, Paris, Bologna or dozens of other universities where basically the same scholarly tasks were being undertaken. It was in this cultural milieu that the theologians again took up the problem of the atonement. With the disappearance of paganism the phenomenon of sacrifice was unknown to ordinary experience, and serious attempts were made to give a rational answer to the perennial questions as to why Jesus died, whether his death was a sacrifice, and how it effected the reconciliation between the human race and God the Father.

For the sake of clarity I will follow the same path as a number of modern writers in classifying the various theories into a number of categories, as a way of coping with the considerable number of explanations which have been advanced for the atonement. The pioneer of this approach was Gustaf Aulén, whose influential study *Christus Victor* has established the pattern for most modern investigations of the whole question.[1] He grouped all the theories into three categories which he called the Classical, the Latin, and the Subjective. The Classical presentation was that of the majority of the Fathers, in Aulén's opinion, and it consisted in expressing the redemptive work of Christ as a victory over the devil. His purpose in writing had been to stress the importance of that approach, which he considered to have been overlooked on account of the wide acceptance of the so-called Latin theory. This was the solution put forward by St Anselm (about which I will say more later), and which was accepted so widely in the Western Church as to obscure the older patristic theory. The third category, the Subjective, was basically liberation by example, namely the heroically inspiring example of Christ's courage in his sufferings.

Some years later Aulén's method was taken up and amplified by Edward Yarnold, who grouped the explanations into four classes.[2] Although close to Aulén's, this grouping is more satisfactory, and it is Yarnold's scheme which I will follow in this chapter. His categories are Atonement as Transaction, Atonement as Conflict, Atonement as Enlightenment, and finally Atonement as Solidarity.[3]

The first of these, Atonement as Transaction, is the same as Aulén's Latin theory, and comprises all those writers who have followed St Anselm. It could be called a forensic explanation of the atonement, and it has had widespread influence ever since it was first propounded in the early Middle Ages. Anselm was one of the outstanding personalities of that period, combining erudition with sanctity and organizational ability. He was born around 1033 in what is now northern Italy, at Aosta. In 1059 he entered the famous Benedictine abbey of Bec in France, and became its abbot in 1078. It has been said of that monastery at that time that it embodied all that was best in the culture of its epoch, like Florence in the early Renaissance, or Athens in the sixth century BC. In 1093 Anselm followed the same path as Lanfranc, the previous abbot of Bec, and became archbishop of Canterbury, where he died in 1109. His most influential book, *Cur Deus Homo,* in which he put forward his theory on the atonement, was completed in 1098, thus keeping alive the tradition that bishops were theologians even in the midst of vast administrative responsibilities or indeed persecution too.

Anselm's solution to the problem of Christ's death and mankind's reconciliation is basically an analogy of the situation of a medieval peasant insulting a king. Reconciliation would not be achieved until satisfaction had been made for the affront to the king's honour. It is no discourtesy to the memory of St Anselm to reflect that he was a child of his time, and lived within the sociological presuppositions of his society. In this perspective, Anselm argued that since Jesus was the son of God, his death had a moral value which was literally unlimited. To be precise it was not so much the death, as the moral excellence of the liberator's love and obedience in accepting the cruel death, which constituted an act of infinite homage to the Father. Thanks to the reality of the incarnation Jesus was authentically a member of the human race, which was henceforth, on balance, more pleasing than displeasing to God. The Father could now welcome back his wayward children without patching up a fictitious reconciliation by merely turning a blind eye to their numerous sins. Indeed to have condoned such wickedness would have been unfitting for a just and all-wise God.

Thus did Anselm present his solution to the vexed question as to why Christ died on the cross.[4] It is basically simple, and provided a rational answer to the fundamental questions as to the purpose of the death of Jesus and its causal role in the moral liberation of the human race. The second advantage is that it is solidly based on the Scriptures, which speak so often and in such diverse ways of the crucifixion as an atoning sacrifice.

Perhaps the greatest advantage of the theory was that it avoided the pitfalls of dealing with the matter in terms of commutative justice. There is no question of the devil having rights over human beings, such as to warrant their being bought back from him. Nor is there any question of human beings inflicting injury to the rights of God by their sins. Strictly speaking, justice and rights can obtain only between equals, and a system of rights does not obtain between God and any of his creatures. Anselm was careful to treat of sin as an affront to the honour of God, and the compensation was not anything like financial repayment of a debt, but what he called 'satisfaction'. This term had been introduced into Latin theology by Tertullian (it is not from the New Testament). It has been defined by Rivière (one of the strongest supporters of Anselm in modern times) as 'Recompense for injured honour, reparation for injury which was inflicted'.[5] It has been defined in slightly less stilted terms by Swinburne as 'voluntary payment of the debt, which overrides the need for punishment'.[6] Personally I prefer Rivière's definition, because he avoids the notions of punishment or payment, both of which are inappropriate, to say the least, in a transaction between Jesus and God the Father.

A further advantage of Anselm's theory is that it cuts the ground from under the allegation that the Father required blood to placate his anger. This view has been popularized by countless writers and preachers, but its most important theological exponent was Harnack. He stated the position quite bluntly in the following words:

The angry God whom it was necessary to propitiate, and of whom the Greeks know so little, became more familiar in the West . . . The distinctive nature, however, of this Latin view of the work of Christ, as the propitiation of an angry God, by a sacrificial death, was characteristically expressed in the firmly established thought that Christ performed it as man, therefore by means not of his divine, but of his human attributes.[7]

There are several points on which one could differ from Harnack, but in the present context it is sufficient to note, with Yarnold, that Anselm had situated the problem in a context which excluded any question of injustice, anger, or revenge.[8]

It is difficult to overestimate the extent of Anselm's influence on subsequent generations. His theory was adopted with only minor modifications by Aquinas,[9] who pointed out that the death of Christ was fitting, but not strictly necessary.[10] The support of Aquinas guaranteed the theory's acceptance within the Catholic Church, but it took hold of the medieval mind so strongly that it was retained in its essentials by the Reformers too. An example of its influence in popular Protestant piety can be seen in the well-known classic *The Pilgrim's Progress*. John Bunyan puts on the lips of one of his characters the following summary of redemption theology, which is clearly no more than a variant on Anselm:

In order to pardon by deed, there must something be paid to God as the price, as well as something prepared to cover us withal. Sin has delivered us up to the just curse of a righteous law: now from this curse we must be justified by way of redemption, a price being paid for the harms we have done, and this is by the blood of your Lord, who came and stood in your place, and stead, and died your death for your transgressions. Thus has he ransomed you from your transgressions by blood, and covered your polluted and deformed souls with righteousness, for the sake of which, God passeth by you and will not hurt you when he comes to judge the world.[11]

By the eighteenth century it had undergone an imperceptible shift at the hands of popular preachers, in the direction of pain. By then, both Catholic and Protestant preachers were stressing the agony of Christ so much that one can understand Harnack's assessment of the atonement as being the appeasement of divine anger.

By the early twentieth century Anselm's theory had become, in practice, the commonly taught solution to the matter among Catholics. Perhaps the most influential Catholic theologian writing on the atonement at that time was Jean Rivière, who published a dozen books on the subject between 1905 and 1948, in addition to the article on Redemption in the influential *Dictionnaire de Théologie Catholique*. He was a faithful follower of the Anselmian school, and considered that the traditional theology of the Church had accepted the notion of satisfaction (following Anselm) as the least unsatisfactory explanation of Christ's redeeming death.[12] In Germany too the theory was widely taught, as can be seen by a glance at such influential textbooks as those of Scheeben and Schmaus.[13]

In spite of its many advantages as a theological explanation, and despite the enormous following among Catholics and Protestants, Anselm's theory is open to serious criticisms. Insofar as it is an explanation of the perennial question as to why Christ had to die on the cross, it is basically an attempt to read into the mind of God, and discern how he manages the relationship with his creatures. One modern writer expressed it succinctly by saying that the Father freely chose to regard the Son's sacrifice as if it were compensation for our sins.[14] Yet it is precisely at this point, of interpreting how God would think and act, that the theory of Anselm displays its most serious weakness. I stated above that the theory was solidly based on the Scriptures. This is true up to a point, but an important distinction must be made. It is perfectly correct that the New Testament speaks of the crucifixion as a sacrifice which has a causative role in liberating us from the consequences of sin. However, as far as reconciliation is concerned, the gospels display a very different picture.

Quite simply, in Jesus' own dealings with sinners and in his teaching about forgiveness, compensation is never required as a prior condition for being received back into the love of God. This is true of the parables of forgiveness, the narratives of conversion or reconciliation of individuals, or in the plain teaching of Christ. Satisfaction is never required as a condition of their being reconciled with God the Father. In recent years this simple, obvious and, to my mind, conclusive objection to Anselm has been put forward by R. Schwager.[15]

There is only one apparent exception, and that is the conversion of Zacchaeus the extortionate tax collector, as recorded in Luke 19:8. He promised to make fourfold restitution to those whom he had swindled. On closer observation it is clear that this was his decision after he had been forgiven by Jesus, not beforehand, and certainly not as a condition imposed by Jesus as the price for his reconciliation. When Peter asked Jesus how often he should forgive his brother (was it to be seven times?), there was no suggestion that he should first of all demand that his brother make satisfaction. 'Seventy times seven' was the answer; there is no question of prior repayment, compensation, or anything similar.[16] So in the spiritual programme presented by Jesus, satisfaction is not required as a precondition for reconciliation. Such being the case, we can have no clearer teaching about the mind of God, and St Anselm's theory, which implies an insight into how God the Father thinks, must be open to serious question. Personally I consider that it is an unanswerable objection to the Anselmian theory of satisfaction.

The second category in Yarnold's classification is that of Atonement as Conflict, and it corresponds to what Aulén had defined as the Classical theory. In general terms it includes all those writers who described the crucifixion as Christ's victory over the devil. In patristic times the atonement was sometimes portrayed as Christ's deceiving the devil, or tricking him (or them), and sometimes as a battle in which Jesus emerged as the victor in spite of the paradoxical event of his being put to death on the cross. Having secured victory in the battle, Christ then brings the mortals out of captivity, like prisoners of war being released at the cessation of hostilities. Aulén gave prominence to this theory because he considered that it had been the classical teaching of Christian antiquity, which had been overshadowed since the Middle Ages by Anselm's theory of satisfaction.

This theory is undoubtedly attractive and can claim among its adherents a thoroughly modern biblical scholar like Martin Hengel, whose description of the crucifixion fits perfectly into this category, as can be seen from the following passage:

In the Son, God himself came to men and was involved in their deepest distress, therein to reveal his love to all creatures. Only as the broken figure on the cross – paradoxically – the exalted one, the Lord, to whom, as God's eschatological plenipotentiary, were subjected even those powers which had apparently triumphed over him at his ignominious death (Philippians 2:6–11; 1 Corinthians 2:8; 2 Corinthians 8:9).[17]

Yarnold introduced minor variations into the theory and speaks of a conflict between God and the forces of evil. This slight shift of language indicates the problem area for the theory as a whole. Admittedly there is much in the New Testament and the writings of the Fathers, not to mention the ancient liturgies, which would legitimize the imagery of a battle between Christ and the devil. But one must bear in mind that the writings in question were basically homilies where the authors employed artistic licence in using perfectly legitimate imagery in order to convey their message forcefully to their hearers. However one has to conclude that when these are stripped of the dramatic imagery, very little substance is left. To put it another way, if we depersonalize the influence of evil, and demythologize the armies of Satan battling under the banners of darkness, or set it all aside as poetic elaboration of the opposition between good and evil, then at the purely rational level little is left of the theory. As Yarnold pointed out, does it reduce to something indistinguishable from Anselm's theory of satisfaction, or merely a powerful expression of the heroic example of Jesus (which is the third category, which I will discuss shortly)?[18]

The Conflict theory has exercised a powerful influence over the Christian imagination. As far as Catholics are concerned this is on account of its having permeated the liturgy. One of the most beautiful hymns of the Latin liturgy is the old Sequence for Easter Sunday, the *Victimae Paschali*:

> Victimae paschali laudes immolant christiani.
> Agnus redemit oves; Christus innocens
> Patri reconciliavit peccatores.
> Mors et vita duello conflixere mirando;
> Dux vitae mortuus regnat vivus.

> To the paschal victim let Christians offer sacrifice of praise.
> The Lamb redeemed the sheep. Christ sinless,
> reconciled sinners to the Father.
> Death and life were locked together in an unique struggle.
> Life's captain died; now he reigns never more to die.[19]

No translation can do justice to the beauty of the Latin text, and when one recalls its plainsong setting the artistic power of this imagery is without equal. It should not surprise us that this manner of describing the liberating work of Jesus has exercised such a powerful influence, in spite of its rational shortcomings.

In spite of the beauty of the hymns and poems which it has inspired, not to mention the vivid imagery of so many sermons, this theory, when stripped of its imagery, does not provide a cogent rational explanation of why Christ had to die and how that death liberated the human race from sin and its consequences.

The third type of theory, which Yarnold calls Atonement as Enlightenment, is roughly the same as Aulén's Subjective class. In an extreme form it was put forward in antiquity by the heretic Pelagius, who held that grace was nothing other than the teaching and example of Christ, thanks to which his followers could overcome sin. This form of the theory commanded no following in the patristic era.

In the Middle Ages, Anselm's contemporary Peter Abelard proposed something similar. In his commentary on the Epistle to the Romans he declared that the redemption was effected by the powerful example of the love which Christ exhibited in his sufferings. Thus human beings were drawn to a life of virtue by persuasion and example, rather than by legal commands as had been the case for the Jews of the Old Covenant.

As there is no readily accessible modern edition of Abelard's commentary on Romans, I will quote a few passages from Migne's nineteenth-century edition. In chapter 2 of the work he states:

It seems to us that our justification in the blood of Christ, and our reconciliation to God, consists in this, namely that we are drawn along by this remarkable grace which has been shown to us, namely that the Son took up our nature and in this nature he persevered up to death, teaching us by word and example . . . Our redemption is therefore that total love of Christ, shown in his passion . . . so that we might fulfil every obligation not by fear but by love of him who showed us grace greater than any that could be found, as he himself has testified.[20]

Abelard's theory commanded no following in the Middle Ages as it was completely overshadowed by the teaching of his contemporary Anselm. However the principle on which it is based has no little appeal, and centuries later something similar was taken up by the German theologian Schleiermacher, who maintained that the sufferings of Christ were not 'redemptional' in the traditional sense. He considered that they gave inspiring example, particularly to people who themselves endure pain and suffering, provided that they are not looked upon as punishment.[21] Since its adoption by Schleiermacher the Exemplar theory has exercised appreciable influence in the twentieth century among both Protestants and Catholics. For example, it seems to be the fairest way to categorize the teaching of Paul Ricoeur. The theme of Christ's painful death occurs in many of his writings. The most recent is his little book *Le Mal*, in which he states simply (in the context of lamentation as a response to suffering):

The theology of the cross, which means the theology according to which God himself died in Christ, signifies nothing other than a transmutation relative to lamentation. The horizon to which that wisdom is pointing seems to me to consist in the renunciation of the desires, even those which are bred of injury seeking redress.[22]

A recent commentator on Ricoeur has come to the same conclusion. After an exhaustive examination of Ricoeur's writings on this matter, K. T. Vanhoozer has presented the question in the context of the quest for freedom, effectively equating redemption and freedom in the thought of Ricoeur. He asks the specific questions about the redemptive work of Jesus in the following words:

How do the gospels change us? The gospels first of all make hope possible. Jesus' passion and resurrection narratives create hope, for they speak of New Being that is stronger and freer than the constraints and limitations of our old ways of being-in-the-world . . . Second, the gospels make freedom possible, because the possibility of freedom is appropriated by the imagination . . . Ricoeur's reading of the passion narrative would have to be classified with what Gustaf Aulén calls the 'subjective' or 'humanistic' type of atonement theology, which sees the significance in terms of its effect on man rather than on God.[23]

The same preference for the Exemplar theory is to be seen also in the theory of one of the most recent Catholic writers, H. E. Mertens, who has given the normal presentation a novel perspective describing the example of Jesus as amounting to 'mastery of the circumstances'. He formulates this theory in an attempt to bypass the dilemma which had been posed by Schillebeeckx, namely as to whether we are saved thanks to, or in spite of, the death of Jesus. His own words are as follows:

The question 'what does the crucified Jesus mean to modern people?' can now be answered. Summarizing, it may be stated that at Golgotha, in spite of the extreme situation of need, Jesus became even more himself through his love – even unto death – for his fellow beings, in faithfulness to his mission from God. His way of dying corresponded to his way of living: turned towards human beings as a consequence of being turned towards Abba, his God. Amidst the absurdity, since the death on the cross was and remains in itself a meaningless event, he behaved meaningfully. His dignified attitude is fascinating. His mastery of circumstances is an example to imitate. Sublimely and infectiously he has demonstrated the historical feasibility of his evangelical call for freedom and shared humanity. Those who have faith in him are stimulated by his example to 'master' even the most painful circumstances and to engage themselves selflessly – despite everything – on behalf of others, thus being in turn enriched themselves . . . The one condemned was not in a position to either change or evade the circumstances, but he was able to master them. Does this model not unlock the real meaning of the 'Ave crux spes unica' (Hail the cross the only hope) (though this really only becomes understandable in the perspective of Easter)? Moreover does this model not allow us to rise above the question 'whether redemption is "in spite of" or "thanks to" Jesus' suffering and death?'[24]

To those rhetorical questions I must answer frankly that it does not convince me that Mertens has bypassed Schillebeeckx's dilemma. A plain reading of the mastery of circumstances indicates that it was thanks to Jesus' death that the example was powerful enough to inspire others. On closer analysis it is not at all clear how the circumstances were mastered. Jesus underwent death like any other victim of ruthless enemies. If it was the resurrection that constituted the essence of mastery, then, without wishing to appear flippant, I can only reflect that modern martyrs cannot count on its occurring three days later, rather than at the end of time. Stripped of a sophisticated presentation, it seems to me that the 'mastery of circumstances' has little to differentiate it from the classical presentation of the Exemplar or Enlightenment models of redemption.

The citations from recent writers indicate that the Exemplar theory of Abelard still has considerable appeal. Perhaps its modern resurgence owes something to the vacuum created by the eclipse of the Conflict theory as well as the Transactional. At the present time many thinkers have totally demythologized the Conflict (or Classical) theory, and even larger numbers find Anselm's forensic type of solution frankly distasteful, if not untenable. As a result the field is open once again for the Exemplar pattern to be viewed with favour. Nevertheless it is open to one insuperable objection, namely that it cannot explain the salvation of those who have not heard the preaching of the gospel, and who cannot have been inspired by the heroic example of Christ.

This brings our enquiry face to face with one of the most vexed questions in the history of theology. In the perspective of this book we must ask: does the work of the atonement benefit people who lived before the time of Christ, or who are totally outside the range of the proclamation of the gospel? Does it reach out to all the members of the human race? Or is it confined to the members of the Christian Churches, who even now are no more than a minority of the world's population? If liberation benefits all people, then some explanation must be found to account for its effect among the non-evangelized, and it cannot be anything reducible to the inspiring example of the life and death of Jesus.

If we are thus to reject the Enlightenment theories of liberation, we must ask very carefully: what are the grounds for advancing the audacious claim that Christ's atoning work was effective for those who would never know of him, in this life?[25]

The first generations of Christians seem to have had no difficulty in accepting the fact that good pagans were saved. The Christians were then a tiny minority of the population and all around them they saw the pagans pursuing their own religious practices. From the psychological point of view they would scarcely have considered that the majority of the population was destined for damnation on account of what they and their ancestors had done in good faith since time immemorial. Such an attitude would have been bred of an arrogance which showed itself among Christians of a much later period, but does not seem to have been present at the beginning. Drawing inspiration from the prologue to St John's gospel, which spoke of the Word of God being in the world since the beginning, they were confident that this Word enlightened all, and they left it at that. Their zeal to share their own belief in Christ was not complicated by a conviction that all other people were damned in the eyes of God.

However in the third century an ominous note was sounded by St Cyprian. When writing about heretics who had left the unity of the Church he formulated the famous maxim *Extra ecclesia nulla salus*.[26] In translating that dictum into English everything hinges upon the rendering of the word *extra*. Is it to be 'Outside the Church there is no salvation' or 'Without the Church there is no salvation'? Roughly speaking, the two translations of that word have determined the lines of this celebrated debate. Cyprian himself, envisaging heretics who had left the Church (in bad faith as he saw it), considered that they had forfeited salvation. It seems unreasonable to extrapolate that judgement to a blanket condemnation of all non-Christians. It would be unfair to attribute to Cyprian this extension of the statement which he formulated for a particular situation, but in later centuries that extension of the principle is exactly what happened.

In medieval Europe Christianity was so widely and firmly established that it seems to have been impossible for the generality of people to understand the religious mentality of non-Christians. On account of the geographical and psychological limitations within which they lived, the people of Europe had little knowledge of other nations and cultures outside their own continent, except perhaps the Muslims, with whom the Crusaders were in contact! The fact that they were universally called 'infidels' tells its own story. Within the confines of Western Europe small Jewish communities were known, and also the occasional heretical movements such as the Albigensians. In conformity with the medieval psychological outlook, both these categories of people were deemed to be excluded from the effects of the liberation because of their presumed contumacious rejection of the Church's mission. It was within the limitations of this outlook that we hear of quaint solutions to the problem of the unevangelized. For example, if a child grew up in a forest away from priests and all other human contact, God would send an angel to preach Christianity to him.

In this period a number of statements from the Church's magisterium lend credence to the exclusive interpretation of the fate of the unevangelized, depending on how one translates the key word *extra* in their texts. In 1215 the Fourth Lateran Council declared *Una vero est fidelium universalis Ecclesia, extra quam nullus omnino salvatur* . . . ('For the universal Church of believers is one, outside [or: without] which no one at all is saved').[27]

A century later the well-known document of Pope Boniface VIII entitled *Unam Sanctam* (after its opening words) made much the same point. The relevant passage is the following:

Unam sanctam Ecclesiam catholicam et ipsam apostolicam urgente fide credere cogimur et tenere, nosque hanc firmiter credimus et simpliciter confitemur, extra quam nec salus est nec remissio peccatorum.

(On the basis of faith we believe in and hold to one holy Catholic and apostolic Church, for ourselves we believe in it firmly and profess it in simplicity, outside [or: without] which there is neither salvation nor remission of sins . . .)[28]

The dogmatic status of that document has been overstressed in the past, and it is important to point out that the authoritative words *declaramus, dicimus, diffinimus* ('we declare, state, define') apply only to the last paragraph of the document, which concerns the authority of the Pope.[29]

On the face of it these two statements appear to favour the strict view about the fate of non-believers, yet it must be remembered that they were drawn up specifically with the Albigensian heresy in mind, and therefore shared basically the same outlook as Cyprian when dealing with heretics who had left the unity of the Church, and who were presumed to be in bad faith. Whether they deserved such an adverse judgement need not detain us here, but it is clear that one cannot extrapolate from a particular historical episode to the generality of people who have had no contact with the preaching of the gospel.

In 1442 similar sentiments were promulgated by the Council of Florence. In the decree for the reconciliation of the Jacobites of Syria, the following sentence is to be found:

Firmiter credit, profitetur, et praedicat nullos extra catholicam Ecclesiam existentes, non solum paganos, sed nec Iudaeos aut hereticos atque schismaticos, aeternae vitae fieri posse participes.

(The Council firmly believes, professes, and preaches that no persons living outside [or: without] the Catholic Church, not only pagans, but neither Jews, heretics, or schismatics can be participants in eternal life.)[30]

Although this statement was promulgated on the authority of the Council of Florence, it was directed to one particular community (the Jacobites): so its doctrinal status has been a matter of dispute. That debate need not detain us here. However it is easy to understand the climate of public opinion within the Church at that time, and it seems that the popular view in the late Middle Ages was that visible incorporation into the community of the Catholic Church was necessary if a person was to benefit from the liberating work of Christ. On such an assumption theories of liberation based on enlightenment, example or subjective factors would be valid; however, just 50 years later one historical event was destined to throw the whole question into the melting pot.

The rather smug consensus about membership of the Catholic Church was shattered for all time in 1492 when the discoveries of Columbus brought home to the Europeans the fact that untold millions of people were alive in places where by no possible stretch of imagination could they have heard the preaching of the Church, or known of the heroic example of Jesus.

This realization opened the debate properly as to the salvation of those outside the area of Christian missionary activity. In modern times the researches of anthropologists, placing the advent of *homo sapiens* further and further back in time, have had a similar effect on the debate. A vast array of theories were put forward and discussed, but for simplicity's sake let me say that the more comprehensive solution to the problem was worked out along the lines of the Church's mediating grace for all people, rather than its preaching to all. In other words, the key phrase coined by St Cyprian was being understood as 'Without the Church there is no salvation'.

For Catholics the matter has been solved by the Second Vatican Council. Although it was not claiming to put forward an irreformable definition on the matter, its statement indicates at least a consensus among Catholic theologians and believers. The relevant statement is to be found in the document on the Church, *Lumen Gentium*:

> Those also can attain to everlasting salvation who through no fault of their own do not know the gospel of Christ or his Church, yet sincerely seek God and, moved by grace, strive by their deeds to do His will as it is known to them through the dictates of conscience. Nor does divine providence deny the help necessary for salvation to those who, without blame on their part, have not yet arrived at an explicit knowledge of God, but who strive to live a good life, thanks to his grace. Whatever goodness or truth is found among them is looked upon by the Church as a preparation for the gospel. She regards such qualities as given by him who enlightens all men that they may finally have life.[31]

The bearing of that statement on the question of the liberating work of Jesus is obvious. Since we can be assured that people who lived before the time of Christ, or outside the range of Christian preaching, do indeed benefit from the salvation earned by Jesus, explanations about his redemptive work must take this fact into account. Any theory which attempts to explain its causality must account for the way in which its effects benefit those who cannot have heard of Jesus, and who cannot have been encouraged by his example. Frankly it is an insuperable difficulty for the Enlightenment theory.

This same theory also has a subsidiary problem, namely it tends to confuse two processes which traditional theology had always considered separately, namely the initial cause of the liberation of the human race from evil, and the subsequent processes by which the spiritual benefits are communicated to individuals. To put it simply, the first does not require a person's consent or even knowledge, but the second stage demands his or her conscious conversion. Admittedly this difficulty is not as great as that presented by the salvation of the unevangelized, but taken together they mean that theories of Enlightenment cannot be sustained.

It is now time to consider the fourth and final category in Yarnold's classification, namely Atonement as Solidarity. This theory is an extension of the doctrine of the Church as the mystical body of Christ, and it means that through contact or solidarity with Christ, what happened to him (resurrection for instance) is communicated to us. The theory draws upon ample backing in the letters of St Paul, and according to Yarnold it is the real meaning of St Paul's numerous phrases like 'in Christ' or 'with Christ'.[32] This theory has affinities with the views of those Greek Fathers who maintained that the incarnation itself was the key to the redemption of the human race, and in which context other events in the life of Jesus such as his crucifixion were somewhat secondary.

However the theory of Solidarity is open to a very serious difficulty: does St Paul envisage this kind of union with Christ (subsequently designated as the Mystical Body) as being with baptized believers, or with the whole human race? Is the Church simply coterminous with humanity? Most studies of the theology of the Mystical Body are agreed that this degree of incorporation into Christ, so as to benefit directly from his redemptive work, is confined to those who have been baptized.[33] The salvation of those who are not in a position to offer explicit faith and receive baptism is upheld by the Church (as I noted above in connection with Vatican II), but there is no unanimity about the channels through which grace comes to them.

It is the clear meaning of St Paul's theology that for baptized believers all manner of spiritual benefits come to them directly as a result of their incorporation into Christ. It is also true that Christ's redemptive work, in the perspective of St Paul, was achieved for the whole human race. But one must not confuse the two categories of people. The spiritual situation of baptized believers is not identical to that of the unevangelized.

The difficulty really arises out of the amalgamation of two parts of the liberating process, which, as I stated above, had been kept separate by traditional theology: the initial earning of redemption by Christ, and the subsequent application of its benefits to the lives of individuals. Admittedly one cannot put the two aspects into watertight compartments, but worse confusion arises from the failure to keep them to some extent distinct. As I pointed out above, the crucial division between the two aspects is that Christ's initial achievement did not require the consent of the human race, but the application to the lives of individuals requires (at least in adults) some measure of conscious acceptance, no matter how diverse their situations may be. The highest degree of conscious collaboration is that of the baptized believer, whose situation may be vastly different from that of the people of good will who have not yet discovered God (to quote the Second Vatican Council).

Another way of expressing the difficulty of the theory of Atonement as Solidarity is to say that it proves too much. It has amalgamated three elements, namely the basic work of Christ earning salvation, the application of this to baptized believers, and its entry into the lives of those who have not known Jesus. Unless the specific requirements of these three processes are borne in mind, none of them will be explained satisfactorily.

Yarnold himself admits some of the limitations of the theory which he favours when he states:

> Although it is not possible to state with any confidence why Christ's achievements can be shared with the rest of the human race . . . it seems to me to be the indispensable basis of the doctrine of the redemption.[34]

In this chapter I have chosen to follow Yarnold's fourfold classification of the theories of the liberation because it provides a scheme within which practically all the attempted solutions stemming from the medieval syntheses can be grouped. It will be apparent from the preceding pages that all four of them have serious weaknesses. For long periods the theories of Atonement as Conflict or as Transaction (St Anselm's, basically) commanded assent among the majority of Christians. This is no longer the case. When examined critically to discover precisely how they explain the causal process by which Christ overcame the effects of sin and thus liberated the human race, they are seen to be defective. Unlike the ancient peoples the modern mind does not automatically accept the efficacity of sacrifices, and unlike our medieval ancestors we do not feel at ease with God's requiring satisfaction prior to reconciliation.

All that is left of the former consensus on this famous question has been reduced to two elements. It is agreed by all Christians that the work of Christ did indeed liberate the human race from sin, and secondly that the Church has not defined any particular theory as being the authentic doctrinal explanation of the matter. Consequently the time would seem to be ripe for seeking a totally different explanation of the causal process implied in the atonement, and this I will attempt to do in the following chapters.

NOTES

1 Gustaf Aulén, *Christus Victor* (London, 1930: reprinted 1965).
2 E. Yarnold, *The Second Gift* (St Paul Publications, Slough, 1974).
3 Yarnold, op. cit., pp. 109ff.
4 Anselm, *Cur Deus Homo*, 1, 19.
5 J. Rivière, *Le Dogme de la Redemption* (Paris, 1931), p. 221.
6 R. Swinburne, *Responsibility and Atonement* (Oxford, 1989), p. 155.
7 A. Harnack, *History of Dogma* (English translation by J. Miller, Edinburgh, 1897), vol. III, Excursus to ch. 6, especially pp. 312, 313.
8 Yarnold, op. cit., p. 112.
9 Aquinas, ST III, q. 48, art. 2.
10 ST III, q. 48, art. 2, ad 1.
11 John Bunyan, *The Pilgrim's Progress*, ed. R. Sharrock (Penguin Classics, London, 1987), p. 272.
12 Rivière, op. cit., pp. 314, 377, 378.
13 M. Scheeben, (French translation) *Les Mystères du Christianisme* (Bruges, 1947), sections 65–68; M. Schmaus, *Katholische Dogmatik*, vol. 2, part 2 (Munich, 1955), pp. 350–61.
14 Yarnold, op. cit., p. 114, interpreting St Anselm.
15 R. Schwager, *Brauchen wir einen Sündenbock?* (Munich, 1978), p. 211.
16 Matthew 18:21, 22.
17 M. Hengel, *The Cross of the Son of God* (London, 1986), p. 74.
18 Yarnold, op. cit., p. 114.
19 Text and translation in J. Connelly, *Hymns of the Roman Liturgy* (London, 1957), p. 86.
20 Abelard, *Commentary on Romans*, II: PL 178, 1836.
21 This estimate of Schleiermacher is accepted by two recent writers on the subject: C. Gunton, *The Actuality of the Atonement* (Edinburgh, 1988), p. 14; and D. L. Wheeler, *A Relational View of the Atonement* (New York, 1990), p. 165.
22 P. Ricoeur, *Le Mal* (Geneva, 1986), p. 25.
23 K. T. Vanhoozer, *Biblical Narrative in the Philosophy of Paul Ricoeur* (Cambridge, 1990), pp. 235, 236.
24 H. E. Mertens, *Not the Cross, But the Crucified* (Louvain, 1992), pp. 173, 174. The reference to Schillebeeckx is to his book *Jesus* (London, 1979), p. 302.
25 Much useful information can still be found in the once standard work on the matter: L. Capéran, *Le Problème du salut des infidèles* (Toulouse, 1934).
26 Cyprian, *Letter* 73, to Jubianus, ed. W. Hartel in *Corpus Scriptorum Ecclesiasticorum Latinorum* (hereafter CSEL; Vienna), vol. 3, part II, p. 778.

27 H. Denzinger, rev. A. Schönmetzer, *Enchiridion Symbolorum, Definitio-num, et Declarationum* (33rd edition; Freiburg, 1965), no. 802 (hereafter referred to as Denzinger).

28 Denzinger, no. 870.

29 Denzinger, no. 875.

30 Denzinger, no. 1351.

31 Vatican II, *Lumen Gentium*, section 16: English translation ed. W. A. Abbott (New York/London, 1966), p. 35.

32 Yarnold, op. cit., p. 118.

33 Cf. E. Mersch, *The Theology of the Mystical Body* (St Louis, 1951), pp. 247–70, and countless other studies on the matter.

34 Yarnold, op. cit., p. 120.

⊠ EXCURSUS TO CHAPTER 4
THE SCAPEGOAT THEME

The fourfold classification of Yarnold, which I followed in Chapter 4, is sufficiently comprehensive to include within its categories virtually all the modern and ancient writers on this subject. However in recent years a new approach has been pioneered which does not fit conveniently into any of the four categories, and which warrants particular treatment. I will explain its development in this excursus.

For some time now it has become apparent that none of the theories hitherto accepted has provided an adequate explanation of how the sins of the human race had been removed so as to bring about reconciliation with God. The precise question as to how the cross caused the liberation has not yet received an answer which the modern mind finds satisfactory. An important new development appeared recently which must be designated as the scapegoat theory, and which transcends the boundaries of any one of Yarnold's four classes.

The theory was inspired by the researches of René Girard, whose influential book *La Violence et le Sacré* appeared in 1972, and was followed six years later by *Des Choses cachées depuis la fondation du monde*.[1]

In both books Girard analyses the role of imitation in human behaviour, which can lead to rivalry and jealousy. Whereas imitation is basically healthy, the tendency to rivalry is dangerous and history shows how devastating are its effects if it gets out of control. It can be restricted through the medium of ritual, which induces a spirit of fear and solidarity.[2] In fact the potential for disaster is so great that rivalry and jealousy can lead on to violence, which can become unlimited and indiscriminate. For this reason societies have had to devise methods to contain violence for their own preservation. Girard maintains that primitive societies channelled the aggressive tendency into sacrificial rites, and the most satisfactory of these was the scapegoat. The Israelite ceremony is a classical example.[3]

The ritual is described in Leviticus 16:21, 22. Two goats were selected; one was sacrificed in the sanctuary and the other was taken by the high priest, who laid his hands on it, symbolizing that he was loading on to it the sins of all the people. It was then driven out into the wilderness, symbolically bearing away the sins of the whole community. This goat was called the goat of Azazel, which was the name of the demon who was believed to inhabit the wilderness. Girard also maintains that of all the world's literature, the New Testament presents the clearest picture of the operation of the scapegoat mechanism.[4]

Girard's theory was taken up by the Austrian theologian Raymund Schwager, who developed the ideas and applied them more precisely to the Christian doctrine of the atonement, in his indispensable book *Brauchen wir einen Sündenbock?*[5] Schwager claims that the scapegoat mechanism is apparent in the suffering Servant of Isaiah chapter 53, which he regards as the high point of the whole of the Old Testament. The Servant takes the anger of God upon himself alone, and thereby deflects it from the Israelite community as a whole. In the New Testament Jesus is depicted as having assumed this role, and he achieves the neutralizing of wickedness by meeting violence with powerlessness. He also makes the point that the New Testament knows of no distinction between lawful and unlawful violence. Both are contrary to the will of God for human beings.[6]

Schwager's important study, which has made a remarkable contribution to the study of soteriology, has one serious drawback. He does not give an altogether clear rational explanation of how the scapegoat mechanism abolished sin and its harmful effects so as to reconcile the human race with God. In the purely sociological context as envisaged by Girard one can understand how the members of a small closely knit community in antiquity could feel the psychological impact of the ceremony, and be purged thereby. When this is extrapolated to the worldwide scale of the human race, something more powerful is needed because we cannot participate in a collective experience of that kind.

Schwager's book was favourably received by the theological reading public. Reviewing it shortly after it appeared, J. B. Bauer exonerated him from being unduly dependent upon Girard, and pointed out that while Girard's work provided a valid basis for a Christian theologian to work from, Schwager had added insights of his own when applying the scapegoat mechanism to the death of Jesus.[7]

In the same year another German theologian, P. Knauer, also reviewed the book favourably, although he had reservations about Schwager's understanding of the response to violence.[8] Schwager followed Girard in maintaining that in order to avert the destructive effects of total war the ancients had canalized their violence on to one individual, the scapegoat. In this perspective Schwager held that Jesus met violence with powerlessness. It was at this point that Knauer felt obliged to differ from him to some extent, namely in pointing out that powerlessness is not the only way in which a Christian can meet violence. In some circumstances a Christian is entitled to resist unjust violence, but Schwager had maintained that the New Testament makes no distinction between justifiable and unjust violence. Nevertheless, Knauer did not dispute the main thesis of Schwager's book.

A perceptive analysis of the works of both Girard and Schwager appeared in 1988 by David B. Burrell.[9] He is favourable to Schwager's thesis, but he points out that in the final analysis his answer to the problem of mankind's collective wickedness is ultimately that of heroic example. To quote Burrell's own words:

The death which he underwent as our scapegoat would empower those who believe in him to live in such a way as to break the round of cover-up through sacrifices so as to reveal things hidden from the foundation of the world (Matthew 13:35).

In other words we are back in the legacy of Abelard, and it is the noble example of Jesus absorbing violence which gives the necessary model for the rest of the believers to do likewise. It seems a fair interpretation of Schwager that his solution to the precise quest being pursued in this book is one of redemption by example. As such it has all the weaknesses inherent in that model of liberation, which I have described in the preceding chapter.

For the next decade Schwager continued to research and write about the atonement. He published ten articles in the *Zeitschrift für Katholische Theologie*, which were assembled eventually into one book entitled *Der wunderbare Tausch*.[10] This was analysed in detail in a long article in *The Thomist* by J. P. Galvin.[11] He notes the influence of Girard on Schwager's work, but does not deny the validity and relevance of his ideas. He points out that Girard had gone so far as to say that the scapegoat mechanism had been devised by the pagans to save society from extinction, since the entailment between imitation, envy, and then violence was so strong. Conflicts had to be resolved before they became totally destructive.

The first six chapters of Schwager's book trace the history of soteriology from the time of Marcion and Irenaeus. Galvin notes that Irenaeus had no adequate theology of the cross. In other words, in his account the crucifixion was not the sole cause of the redemption. When dealing with those Fathers who wrote in terms of conflict with the devil, Schwager's updating of the idea for the modern reader was to say that the opposition to Jesus was the operation of collective forces of human envy which were unmasked by Jesus' non-retaliatory stance in the face of violence. When evaluating Schwager's treatment of Gregory of Nyssa, Galvin observes that for Gregory the incarnation itself was the basic cause of the redemption, and consequently he too lacked an adequate theology of the cross. This point is worth noting, as I will have more to say about its implications when I present my own theory. Schwager's treatment of Pelagius is perceptive. He had taught that the human race is invited to follow the example of Christ's heroic death; but this is virtually self-redemption, and St Augustine, not surprisingly, disputed it from the standpoint of the necessity of grace.

Schwager's treatment of Maximus the Confessor illustrates the persistent problems which had beset all theories of the liberation. Christ's saintly life and heroic death acted like leaven in the dough, thereby affecting the whole human race for the better. However Maximus does not tell us exactly how this holy fermentation actually operated, and that is the precise question to which the modern mind seeks an answer. Schwager concludes the patristic section of his book by observing that all the Fathers were hampered in their theorizing by their limited view of Christ's freedom. In all fairness it must be pointed out that Maximus, in the face of the monothelite heresy, had upheld the existence in Jesus of a human free will. However he and his predecessors had been inhibited from exploring the extent of that freedom on account of their belief that Jesus enjoyed the beatific vision throughout his earthly life.

A partial solution to the difficulty about Christ's freedom was supplied by St Anselm, which gave him an advantage over his predecessors, since Anselm is quite clear on the point that Christ was able to choose between the good and the better. For all its limitations it was a realistic concept of freedom. In all fairness to Anselm we must remember that it is only in recent years that theologians have come to terms with the full extent of Christ's freedom, thanks to their having absorbed a great deal from psychology and its allied sciences. But, as Schwager reminds us, we are all indebted to Anselm because, like the moderns, he did seek a truly rational solution to the problem of what caused the atonement.

The limitations of Anselm's theory have been dealt with in the previous chapter, and I find Schwager's development of Anselm's ideas no more satisfactory. To quote his own words: 'Free personal decisions not only determine one's own will, but also co-determine intrinsically the will of others', and later on, 'Christ's love which climaxed on the cross, once for all re-established human willing, heretofore weakened and bound by a history of sin'.[12] Statements like these, which have echoes of the preacher's paradox, may be very effective in homilies, but do not supply the rational answers to the crucial questions as to how the redemption was actually brought about.

Der wunderbare Tausch has received more adverse criticism than did Schwager's earlier book on the subject. The French theologian B. Sesboué, himself the author of a book on the subject, reviewed it somewhat negatively. In fact he questioned the suitability of employing Girard's categories for the supernatural work of the redemption.[13] Much the same judgement was made by A. Louth, who considered that Schwager was insufficiently critical in his use of Girard's theory, although he did not deny its suitability in this context.[14]

Schwager himself considers that more research into contemporary theology and other disciplines is necessary before a comprehensive theology of salvation can be attempted.[15]

The scapegoat theory found a congenial home in the novel and original perspectives of Hans Urs von Balthasar's *Theodramatik*. He studies a number of basic themes in the world's classical dramas in order to draw upon their significance for theology. Not surprisingly, he took up the scapegoat mechanism sympathetically. In contrast to some other readers of Girard and Schwager, he agrees that the scapegoat mechanism can be of valid assistance in understanding the phenomenon of sin and its remedy. The Christian use of the imagery cannot stay within the limitations of the original ceremony. He remarks that Jesus, unlike other scapegoats, did not have the sins laid on him without his consent, but it is most important to bear in mind that he took them upon himself willingly.[16]

The central paradox of what took place on the cross is expressed by von Balthasar in these words:

> The drama between humanity and God achieved here its acme, since the perverse and ultimate freedom transfers all its guilt on God as the unique culprit and scapegoat. God allows himself to become involved therein not only in the humanity of Christ but also in the trinitarian mission of the Son. So in the mysterious darkening and estrangement between God and the sin bearing Son, as the unique point of the representative substitution, the almighty powerlessness of the love of God shines out: what was experienced is the opposite of what happened in fact.[17]

The paradox which he is describing is the contrast between Christ's apparent total abandonment by the Father as if he were unloved and powerless, whereas it was this very abasement which produced the most powerful operation of the love of the Father for humanity, in bringing back the whole human race into reconciliation with himself. Precisely how it was achieved he does not say. It seems fair to von Balthasar to accept that he considered that it was inevitably mysterious. In fact he quotes Vincent Turner in that sense as confirmation of his own view. Von Balthasar's quotation from Turner is taken from Turner's commentary on Mark, after the words 'My God my God, why hast thou forsaken me?', and he explains:

> The view maintained by Lutheran and Reformed theologians . . . that Jesus, as a substitute for sinners was forsaken by the Father is inconsistent with the love of God . . . The depths of the saying are too deep to be plumbed, but the least inadequate interpretations are those which find in it a sense of the desolation in which Jesus felt the horror of sin so deeply that for a time the closeness of his communion with the Father was obscured.[18]

Bearing in mind these various estimates of the scapegoat mechanism, it seems reasonable to conclude that either they have left the causality ultimately as a mystery, or else they have remained within the main lines of the exemplary or subjective theories. The latter group, despite their remaining within the limitations of Abelard's insight, have made one important advance. They have drawn attention to the fact that in the teaching and example of Jesus, violence and injustice are to be met with endurance and powerlessness, not with alternative violence as a form of opposition. It is an important precision, and is of value to this generation which has come to appreciate the strength and effectiveness of non-violent protest against injustice. Although my own solution to the whole problem of the atonement is different from that of the exemplar models, I accept the importance of the heroic example of Christ's non-violent stance in the face of his arrest and execution.

NOTES

1 R. Girard, *La Violence et le Sacré*, translated into English as *Violence and the Sacred* (Baltimore, 1977) and *Things Hidden Since the Foundation of the World* (London, 1987).
2 Girard, *Things Hidden*, p. 284.
3 Girard, *Violence and the Sacred*, p. 99.
4 Girard, *Things Hidden*, p. 131.
5 R. Schwager, *Brauchen wir einen Sündenbock?* (Munich, 1978); translated into English as *Do We Need Scapegoats?* (Baltimore, 1987).
6 Schwager, *Brauchen wir einen Sündenbock?*, p. 179.
7 J. B. Bauer, reviewing Schwager, *Theologische Revue* (1978), p. 383.
8 P. Knauer, reviewing Schwager, *Theologie und Philosophie* (1978), pp. 564–6.
9 D. B. Burrell, 'René Girard: violence and sacrifice', *Cross Currents* (1988), pp. 446–8.
10 R. Schwager, *Der wunderbare Tausch* (Munich, 1986); translated into English as *The Marvellous Exchange* (1988).
11 J. P. Galvin, '*The Marvellous Exchange*: Raymund Schwager's interpretation of the history of soteriology', *The Thomist* (1989), pp. 675–91.
12 Galvin, art. cit., p. 685.
13 B. Sesboué, reviewing *Der wunderbare Tausch*, *Recherches de Science Religieuse* (1989), p. 544.
14 A. Louth, reviewing *Der wunderbare Tausch*, *Journal of Theological Studies* (1989), pp. 703–5.
15 Galvin, art. cit., p. 689.
16 H. Urs von Balthasar, *Theodramatik* (Einsiedeln, 1980), vol. 4, p. 311.
17 Von Balthasar, op. cit., p. 312.
18 V. Turner, *The Gospel according to St Mark* (London, 1952), p. 594; quoted in von Balthasar, op. cit., p. 312 note.

5

⊠ *Towards a solution*

In the preceding chapters I have often spoken about reconciliation. The time has come to state more precisely what is meant by
this notion. In the context of salvation it is concerned with
repairing the damage done by sin, and in the past this was viewed
in terms of the infringement of rules or laws, and their subsequent
integral observance. This approach has obvious limitations, and I
prefer to consider the whole matter in terms of personal relationships. In this context I would describe reconciliation as the
rebuilding of a relationship of love and trust which had been
destroyed by some form of infidelity or exploitation. Expressed in
those terms it can apply to the interaction between human beings,
and to their intimacy with, or estrangement from, God.

A remarkable instance of the significance and profundity of the
matter was supplied by Donald Nicholl, describing the situation in
the former Soviet Union since the discrediting of Stalinism. His
remarks arose out of reflections on the visit to England of a Soviet
peace delegation in 1988.

I recalled the most unforgettable conversation I have had during the past year.
My interlocutor was Ales Adamovich, a member of the small Soviet peace
delegation which visited London last November. Knowing how vigorously
Adamovich has been campaigning to cleanse Soviet society of the poison of
Stalinism, I asked him whether it would be true to say that probably one in
three people of my own age in the Soviet Union (that is, people in their sixties)
had at some time denounced a fellow citizen. And if so, however can a society
be cleansed whose members are so deeply poisoned? Adamovich agreed that
my estimate might well be correct. He added that he was less worried by those
Soviet citizens who oppose glasnost than by those who had fallen in with
Stalinism and Brezhnev in the past, yet nowadays voiced their support for
glasnost. Such people he said simply make an adjustment; but they do not do

repentance, which is something quite different. Through adjustment you finish up with exactly the same counters available to you as before, but arranged in a different pattern, whereas through repentance genuine newness emerges, and unsuspected possibilities open up.[1]

I trust that the above quotation makes clear that reconciliation is a realistic concept; in fact it is vital to life, as can be seen if one ponders on the unremitting cycle of violence, hatred and revenge which has blighted the whole of human history. Estimates vary, but it may be that there have been at least 120 wars since the end of the Second World War. The number varies depending upon how one defines a war. Civil war can break out unexpectedly, for instance in Yugoslavia in 1992, because there never has been reconciliation between communities who inflicted injuries on one another hundreds of years ago.

Repentance or conversion is the first stage in rebuilding a shattered relationship, and it applies to the reconciliation between men or between humans and God.

The next stage in our enquiry is to try to appreciate something of the sheer magnitude of the undertaking which is involved in reconciling the human race with God. Here one's imagination is stretched to its utmost limits, because what is at stake is a virtual mountain of sin, guilt, and general moral badness, which must be remedied somehow, so as to bring together countless millions of wayward human beings with the infinite God. Both parties to this reconciliation are in their own ways so vast as to defy comprehension.

In the preceding chapters I have indicated that in the process of counteracting the damage which had separated mankind from God, neither compensation, nor satisfaction, nor anything similar was required. If reparation is not demanded, what exactly is required as the first step towards rebuilding the broken relationship? On this matter the teaching of Jesus is unambiguously clear: forgiveness must be asked for. Nothing more nor less is required than the sinner's requesting readmission to the love of God, or reconciliation with his brother. Perhaps the concept is deceptively simple. Be that as it may. The gospels leave no doubt about this plain fact: compensation is not required in any form, but reconciliation must be asked for specifically and deliberately. This is the crucial insight which Raymund Schwager has brought to the study of soteriology, and which has opened a new chapter in the development of this branch of theology.[2]

One could cite practically the whole of the gospels in support of this contention, but the best-known instances are the following, which I will refer to in the traditional sequence of the gospels, for the sake of simplicity.

Jesus eats with sinners and tax collectors at a feast after the calling of Levi, and tells his critics that he has come to call sinners and not the virtuous (Matthew 9:13 and Mark 2:17). They had not been required to pay compensation before Jesus joined them at table. The parable of the lost sheep (Matthew 18:12) conveys the same message. The shepherd made no prior conditions before setting out in search of it. When Peter asked if he should forgive his brother seven times (Matthew 18:21) the answer was not about satisfaction, but merely that on request he must forgive seventy times seven. The parable of the unforgiving debtor is even clearer (Matthew 18:23–35) because the central figure did require compensation from his debtor, while being offered unconditional forgiveness himself, merely on request. The paralytic who was lowered through the roof (Mark 2:1–12) was not only cured, but also had his sins forgiven without any prior conditions. The dramatic approach had made his intentions clear. The sinful woman who anointed the feet of Jesus as he reclined at a banquet (Luke 7:36) was forgiven simply on the strength of her expressive gesture of love. The famous parable of the prodigal son (Luke 15:11–32) emphasizes the principle most clearly of all, because the situation so obviously called for a repayment to his father of the squandered money. No such thing was required by the forgiving father. The case of Zacchaeus the repentant tax collector (Luke 19:1–10) is an apparent exception because he promised fourfold restitution. Yet as I pointed out earlier, when dealing with St Anselm's theory, Zacchaeus had been reconciled with Christ before making the promise of restitution. It had not been exacted as the price of forgiveness. The good thief on the cross (Luke 23:39–43) made a simple request for acceptance and was promised paradise without more ado. The narrative of the woman taken in adultery (John 8:1–11) is of questionable authenticity because of its absence from a number of ancient manuscripts. It shows the attitude either of Jesus, or of some of his early followers who inserted it into the text of the fourth gospel. Either way it is an example of unconditional forgiveness. Peter's threefold profession of his love of Jesus (John 21:15–19) is usually understood as being a disavowal of his threefold denial, and indicates yet again that sincere dispositions are required for reconciliation, and not any form of antecedent penance or satisfaction.

In case this reduction of reconciliation to the simple request for forgiveness should look like an easy option, let me remind my readers of what Bonhoeffer said: there is no such thing as cheap grace. The examples from the gospels which I quoted in the preceding paragraph may have been simple in one sense because they were uncomplicated, but all of them represented deep sincerity. They were not superficial, nor did they trivialize the importance of what was at stake. For all of the central figures it entailed virtually a life's conversion. It is rather like the case of Naaman the Syrian. He did not believe that Elisha could cure him unless the prophet performed an extravagant ritual. Bathing in the river, at the behest of the prophet, seemed to him too simple a way of canalizing the power of God.[3] Asking for forgiveness is the same. The dialogue is simple, but what is entailed is profound. The sinner has resolved to change his course of life, and that is what is implied in the request for forgiveness when it is sincerely made.

It is worth noting that this simple requirement, of repentance and nothing more, is not confined to the teaching of Jesus. We read of it in the Old Testament too, where God is calling back Israel to fidelity.[4] Since the drama of infidelity and repentance between Israel and God lies somewhat outside the scope of this book, I will confine myself to the teaching of Jesus in the New Testament. The lesson is clear from the examples which I have quoted. It is also constant: if individuals are to be forgiven and reconciled to God, they must ask for this with sincerity. Moral conversion is the only prerequisite. No form of satisfaction, penance or compensation is required as a prior condition of acceptance back into a loving relationship with God.

If we are attempting to understand the mind of God, then we have it here. In the previous chapter I pointed out that St Anselm and his followers were endeavouring to understand how God's mind worked in the matter of reconciliation. They considered that the deity would require satisfaction as the price for being reconciled with the human race. This appeared to fit neatly into the scheme of regarding the crucifixion as the price, which was their understanding of those references to it in the epistles. In fact they were wrong. Every instance in the teaching and activity of Jesus where forgiveness is sought shows that individuals are welcomed back to the love of God if they merely ask for it sincerely. On this basis we are entitled to state that if God wishes to reconcile the human race to himself, the same principle applies to the collectivity as to the individuals, and the human race must ask for forgiveness. Theoretically the request might have been made by countless individuals petitioning on their own behalf. In fact it has been done for all of us by Jesus. Acting as the spokesman for the whole human race he has requested the reconciliation for us all. Basically nothing more or less is required for the atonement.

In case this assertion should appear either as deceptively simple or as a gross overstatement of reality, it is important to analyse just what is entailed in the task of acting as authentic spokesman for the human race. One thing is perfectly clear: the concepts of atonement and the work of a liberator are relevant and meaningful for the twentieth century. It is the method which is in question for our contemporaries. In a parallel context Wolfhart Pannenberg has said of the concepts entailed in Jesus' redemptive death that 'they are neither unhistorical superimpositions nor untenable for contemporary thought, but historically sound and meaningful for the present'.[5] The difficulty of grasping the significance of the operation arises out of the fact that there is on the one hand what could be described as an ocean of unfathomable badness. On the other hand there is the God who is infinite, and with whom we are to be reunited in love. By what process does anyone acquire competence to speak on behalf of so many millions as their representative? The simple answer is that Jesus in his role as Messiah was the spokesman not merely for the Jews, but for the whole of humanity. Although his contemporaries were slow to acknowledge the calling of the gentiles, it is clear in the psalms and the prophets that in the messianic age the other nations would also be invited to repent and to come to worship the true God. It was the most important lesson which the early community had to learn, namely to extend the New Covenant to the non-Jews, and it is related with great emphasis in the Acts of the Apostles.

I will leave to one side the detailed processes by which individuals take up this comprehensive welcome, and I will leave to the next chapter an analysis of how and when Jesus did the asking. For the moment I will limit myself to the fundamental matter of his competence to be the authentic spokesman for all human beings, such that he could genuinely speak on behalf of the whole human race. It is important that we can grasp it realistically, and discuss it without simply lapsing into metaphor. Obviously the reader will have perceived the magnitude of the undertaking which we attempt to analyse meaningfully.

At one level Jesus' role as Messiah arose from his being born into the Israelite nation, thus sharing their whole biological and spiritual destiny. His designation as Messiah was indicated by the divine communications to Mary, Joseph, and others around the time of his birth. The divine commission to act as Messiah can reasonably be located in the mysterious happening when he was baptized by John in the Jordan. His call from God was similar to that of the prophets. Suddenly and without prior training or preparation, they received their extraordinary vocation, which seems to have been in practice more or less irresistible. From that point onwards they spoke in the name of God, delivering his message whether they or the hearers liked it or not. The start of Jesus' messianic mission was much the same.

At a deeper level his role as Messiah and spokesman for the other nations is rooted in the incarnation. The first element in this understanding of his role is his humanity. Fundamentally he was qualified to speak on behalf of the human race because he was a member of it, sharing with us all human characteristics except sin. After two thousand years of Christian history this may seem so obvious as to be a mere truism. However the point was not lost on the first heretics. The earliest detectable heretical movement, the Docetists, denied the reality of his human body. The reaction of the infant Church was an immediate affirmation of his true humanity, because they realized that it was essential to his mission. The problem did not occur again. In the fourth and fifth centuries the question of the human nature of Jesus arose in theological disputes, not in its own right, but in relation to the hypostatic union. In other words, by what kind of connection was the true human nature of Jesus linked to the divine Word, the second person of the Trinity. In this context and in slightly different ways the Councils of Ephesus (431) and Chalcedon (451) declared that the human nature of Jesus was complete, perfect, and the same as our own in all things except sin.[6]

A further element in Christ's role as spokesman for the whole of humanity also arises out of the incarnation, and it is one aspect of the power possessed by his human nature in virtue of its intimate union with the divinity. Unlike an ambassador or trade union negotiator (to use everyday examples), Christ was not appointed or elected to the task in any contingent sense. His competence flowed automatically as a consequence of the hypostatic union. It did not arise suddenly in the mysterious theophany at his baptism. That was merely the triggering into action of his public mission. Aquinas spoke of something very similar in his treatment of the Church as the mystical body of Christ. He stated that the whole humanity of Christ, body and soul, had the power to impart grace to human beings in virtue of the union between that particular human nature and the divine Word of God.[7] The matter has been developed at length by modern theologians writing about the Church as the mystical body of Christ.[8] Aquinas and his commentators were studying what could be described in simple terms as the flowing of grace within the mystical body, coming from Christ to the men and women who make up the Church. As such they presupposed the accomplishment of the liberating process, and envisaged the situation where the Church could be considered as functioning normally in the historical period after the ascension. Without wishing to appear pedantic, I intend to suggest a distinction for the sake of clarity. I think that it is legitimate to make at least a logical distinction between the accomplished work of salvation and the basis from which Christ derived his competence as liberator. It is my contention that prior to the crucifixion and resurrection he was competent to act as spokesman for the human race in virtue of his divinity, and to do so precisely because he was its creator. Admittedly his authority flows directly from the divinity of the Son of God, but his exact relationship with the human race is brought into clearer perspective when we advert to the fact that he was its creator initially. This is the overall context of his relationship with the whole universe, and more precisely with its human inhabitants.

Theology has conserved two ways of presenting Christ in the process of creation. In the Middle Ages and under the influence of Greek philosophy it was generally stated that operations of the Persons of the Trinity in relation to the 'outside world' were common to all three of them. In this view the Son of God can be considered as sharing in the creation of the universe in the same way as the other two persons of the Trinity, who all operated through the divine nature which is considered as the source of the operation, if one may express the matter in such words.

The second way of understanding creation is the more nuanced presentation in the New Testament. In the prologue to St John's gospel we read that the Word of God was present in the beginning, and that all things were made through him (*panta di'autou egeneto*) (John 1:2-3). The same idea is expressed in the letter to the Colossians (1:15-16) where St Paul described the Son's role in creation thus: 'He is the image of the invisible God, the first born of all creation; for in him all things were created, in heaven and on earth.' More or less the same concept is to be found in Hebrews 1:1-2: 'In many and various ways God spoke of old to our fathers by the prophets; but in these last days he has spoken to us by a Son, whom he appointed the heir to all things, through whom also he created the world.' The same thought underlies Hebrews 2:10: 'For it was fitting that he, for whom and by whom all things exist, in bringing many sons to glory, should make the pioneer of their salvation perfect through suffering.' It lies outside the scope of this book to pursue the ramifications of those two presentations of the doctrine of creation. As far as the present study is concerned, it is clear that the Son of God is related to the universe (and thence to the human race) as its creator. No more powerful title to competence could be envisaged in enquiring as to his credentials as spokesman for that same human race in its relationship to God the Father.

As a consequence of his place within the Trinity, and thanks to the incarnation, Jesus is truly human and paradoxically creator of the human race. Christ the Messiah is competent to speak for humanity in asking for reconciliation between mankind and God the Father. In short he is the intercessor or mediator. This competence was his from the moment of the incarnation, before he had undergone the sufferings of his passion, and had been glorified in the resurrection.

This concept is so profound and important to the process of liberation that one must pause and ask: is the whole notion just an artificial creation of theologians' sophistry, or is it germane to the pattern of God's dealings with the human race as shown in the Bible? It is an important question to ask because the intricacies of this role as deriving from the incarnation might seem to bear the mark of an artificially contrived theory. Fortunately for our reassurance there is adequate precedent for the role of intercessor in the mainstream of the Old Testament, namely in the person of Moses, and to a lesser extent Abraham. Hebrew has no exact word for 'intercessor' or for 'mediator', but the function was clear, as the following instances will show.

Abraham's role as intercessor is best known on account of the charming narrative of his pleading for the cities of Sodom and Gomorrah:

Then the Lord said, 'Because the outcry against Sodom and Gomorrah is great and their sin is very grave, I will go down to see whether they have done altogether according to the outcry which has come to me; and if not I will know.' So the men turned from there, and went towards Sodom; but Abraham still stood before the Lord. Then Abraham drew near, and said, 'Wilt thou indeed destroy the righteous with the wicked? Suppose there are fifty righteous within the city; wilt thou then destroy the place and not spare it for the fifty righteous who are in it? Far be it from thee to do such a thing, to slay the righteous with the wicked . . .' And the Lord said, 'If I find at Sodom fifty righteous in the city I will spare the whole place for their sake.' . . . 'Suppose ten are found there?' He answered 'For the sake of ten I will not destroy it.' And the Lord went his way, when he had finished speaking with Abraham; and Abraham returned to his place. (Genesis 18:20–33)

The preservation of the cities at the request of Abraham is an authentic example of intercession, but there are more and indeed clearer instances of that role in the life of Moses, who ranks as the intermediary *par excellence* in the Old Testament.[9] In the Book of Exodus he is depicted as interceding for Pharaoh and the Egyptians in securing the cessation of the plague of frogs (Exodus 8:8–13, 28–31). He interceded on their behalf to secure the cessation of the plague of thunder and hail (Exodus 9:27–33), and similarly in the case of the plague of locusts (Exodus 10:16–19). He interceded on behalf of Aaron after the making of the golden calf: 'And the Lord was so angry with Aaron that he was ready to destroy him; and I prayed for Aaron also at the same time' (Deuteronomy 9:20, recording Moses speaking in the first person). Miriam too benefited from the intercession of Moses after she had been punished with leprosy on account of her opposition to Moses: 'Moses cried to the Lord "Heal her O God I beseech thee"' (Numbers 12:13).

Somewhat more to the purposes of this study are the instances where Moses interceded for the whole people of Israel. This happened after the giving of the Covenant on Mount Sinai, when the people as a whole showed their infidelity by worshipping the molten calf. As a punishment God threatened to destroy them, but Moses prayed on their behalf:

'O Lord why does thy wrath burn hot against thy people whom thou hast brought forth out of the land of Egypt with great power and with a mighty hand? Why should the Egyptians say "With evil intent did he bring them forth, to slay them in the mountains, and consume them from the face of the earth"? Turn from thy fierce wrath, and repent of this evil against thy people. Remember Abraham, Isaac, and Israel, thy servants to whom thou didst swear by thine own self, and didst say to them, "I will multiply your descendants, and they shall inherit it for ever." ' And the Lord repented of the evil which he thought to do to his people. (Exodus 32:11–14)

The same incident is also recorded in Deuteronomy 9:18–29.

The people sinned again after receiving the gift of manna (Numbers 11:11–25). They showed their ingratitude by their longing for meat. This narrative is complicated, as it serves as the occasion for the appointing of the seventy elders, who in turn also needed the intercession of Moses on account of their jealousy of the two men who had received the Spirit although they were outside the group of elders.

The incidents surrounding the return of the spies who had reconnoitred the promised land provide explicit statements about sin, threatened punishment, and the efficacy of the intercession of Moses. The reports of the spies were discredited by the people, who feared the perils of the campaign of conquest. The narrative continues:

The Lord said to Moses, 'How long will this people despise me? And how long will they not believe in me, in spite of all the signs which I have wrought among them? I will strike them with the pestilence and disinherit them . . .' But Moses said to the Lord ' . . . Pardon the iniquity of this people I pray thee, according to the greatness of thy steadfast love, and according as thou hast forgiven this people, from Egypt even until now.' Then the Lord said 'I have pardoned according to your word.' (Numbers 14:11–20)

After the rebellion of the sons of Korah, God threatened to destroy the nation, but at the prayer of Moses the punishment was limited simply to the guilty ones (Numbers 16:20–24).

The last incident which I will cite is that of the fiery serpents (most probably scorpions or snakes). The people had grown weary of eating manna, and were complaining about the general discomfort of life in the desert. As a punishment they were visited by a plague of fiery serpents, at which point they sought the intercession of Moses:

And the people came to Moses and said, 'We have sinned, for we have spoken against the Lord and against you; pray to the Lord that he may take away the serpents from us.' So Moses prayed for the people. And the Lord said to

Moses, 'Make a fiery serpent, and set it upon a pole; and everyone who is bitten, when he sees it, shall live.' So Moses made a bronze serpent and set it on a pole; and if a serpent bit any man, he would look at the bronze serpent and live. (Numbers 21:7–9)

From the information in the foregoing quotations about Abraham and Moses it is possible to clarify the notion of a mediator or spokesman as it was understood in the Old Testament. It makes little difference to the argument if the incidents have been embellished by later editors in the light of more sophisticated theological reflection. Since it is the mediation of Jesus which concerns us, it is the understanding of that role among his contemporaries which is relevant. That understanding was formed by the Old Testament as we have it now, a form acquired several centuries before the time of Jesus.

Moses was competent to be the intercessor or spokesman firstly because he was of the race of Israel. He lived among them and shared their sufferings in Egypt. God designated him as their leader, and his leadership role was greater than that of any subsequent head of the nation, even King David. It was his responsibility to lead them out of slavery into the liberation of the promised land. But, more importantly, on the religious plane he was empowered to receive and ratify the Covenant on their behalf. It was the Covenant which constituted their unique status among the nations of the world, in their special relationship with God, which institutionalized their religion on the basis of the self-disclosure of the true God. Thus he was competent for all dialogue and communication between the people and their God. In this context his requests for the forgiveness of their sins fitted in quite naturally. It set the pattern for the mediatorial role of Jesus.

It has been suggested that there is a third important mediator in the Old Testament, namely the suffering Servant of Deutero-Isaiah.[10] His role as intercessor is spoken of explicitly in Isaiah 53:12, after the announcement of the Servant's death:

Therefore I will divide him a portion with the great, and he shall divide the spoil with the strong; because he poured out his soul to death, and was numbered with transgressors; yet he bore the sins of many, and made intercession for transgressors.

I have argued elsewhere in this book that the death of the Servant was an important stage in developing the theology of vicarious atonement in Jewish thought. Undoubtedly it prepared the ground for the realization in the time of Jesus that the deaths of martyrs could be considered as sacrifices atoning for other people's sins. The role of mediator or intercessor includes the two aspects of suffering for others and also asking for their reconciliation with God. I do not think that it is possible to argue for more than an atoning death in the case of the Servant in Isaiah. It is not clear that he interceded verbally like Moses for the reconciliation of the people with God.

On the strength of what the Old Testament taught about Abraham and Moses, it is clear that the notion of an intercessor who asks for reconciliation between the people and God is germane to the Bible. When it is applied to Jesus it cannot be argued that such an identification is artificial. There is moreover one further link in the chain which strengthens the designation of Jesus as the intercessor, namely the deliberate depicting of Jesus as the second Moses in St Matthew's gospel.

The theory was first advanced in 1930 by B. W. Bacon,[11] and has been debated at length ever since.[12] The arguments in favour of such a depicting of Jesus can be summarized as follows. The discourses of Jesus are grouped into five artificially arranged long speeches, each of which ends with almost identical words, 'When Jesus finished these sayings.'[13] This would suggest a clear imitation of the five books of Moses. Similarly, the ten miracles of Matthew 8:1 – 9:34 seem to be presented as a parallel to the ten plagues of Egypt. The long discourse known as the Sermon on the Mount (Matthew 5:1ff.) took place on what Luke specifically designates as flat ground (Luke 6:17). Matthew insinuates that it was reminiscent of Mount Sinai. The narrative of the infancy of Moses must surely have been the model for the recording of the infancy of Jesus, and the desire of Herod to kill Jesus bears a significantly close resemblance to the wording of Pharaoh's intention to kill Moses. The words used to declare that it was safe to return home are almost identical in both instances (Exodus 4:19; Matthew 2:20). Undoubtedly the basic inspiration for this identification is to be found in Deuteronomy 18:15, where Moses is quoted as saying: 'The Lord your God will raise up for you a prophet like me from among you, from your brethren, him you shall heed.'

The cumulative force of these arguments is impressive, particularly if one bears in mind the fact that allusion was then used where a modern writer would have made a specific identification. The method and its application have been studied extensively. R. Laurentin applied it to the infancy narrative in Luke.[14] One example from Laurentin's work will show how effective was that allusive method when properly understood. In Luke 1:56 it is stated that Mary remained with her kinswoman Elizabeth for about three months. The significance of that length of time was lost on commentators for centuries. Laurentin pointed out that it is a verbatim quotation from 2 Samuel 6:11 where the Ark of the Covenant remained in the house of Obededom for three months. It was Luke's way of speaking about the incarnation, and the presence of God in the house of Elizabeth.[15] Once this method is understood it will be seen that what is obscure to the twentieth-century non-Semitic reader would have been transparently clear to St Matthew's contemporaries.

As the matter is still disputed among New Testament scholars, I feel that it is prudent to cite the opinion of Joachim Jeremias on this subject:

In sum it may be said that the Moses–Christ typology did not exercise a central or controlling influence on New Testament christology. Nevertheless whether explicit or implicit, whether with emphasis on points of comparison or points of contrast, it is almost everywhere expressed in the New Testament and it is one of the motifs which helped to shape New Testament christology. Moses and Christ are the two divine messengers of the Old Covenant and the New. They are linked by the same fate of rejection and misunderstanding.[16]

In the light of all that has been stated in this chapter it seems beyond all reasonable doubt that we are entitled to regard Christ as the intercessor for the human race, who is competent to act as our spokesman, seeking reconciliation with God on behalf of all mankind. The role has been deduced by theologians as a direct consequence of the incarnation, and this conclusion is consonant with the biblical background. When, where and how Jesus performed the work of intercession I will deal with in the next chapter.

NOTES

1 Donald Nicholl in *The Tablet* (1 July 1989), p. 749.
2 R. Schwager, *Brauchen wir einen Sündenbock?* (2nd edition; Munich, 1986), p. 211, and several other places in the book.
3 2 Kings 5:9–14.
4 Hosea 14:2–9 etc.

5 Wolfhart Pannenberg, quoted in Herbert Nele, *The Doctrine of the Atonement in the Theology of Wolfhart Pannenberg* (Berlin, 1970), p. 136.

6 Council of Ephesus: Denzinger no. 264; Council of Chalcedon: Denzinger no. 301.

7 Aquinas, ST III, q. 8, art. 2, also arts 1 and 5.

8 Cf. M. Scheeben, *Mysterien des Christentums*, sections 65–68: English translation *The Mysteries of Christianity* (St Louis and London, 1947), pp. 431–65; E. Mersch, *Le Corps Mystique du Christ* (Brussels, 1951), pp. 214–18; English translation *The Whole Christ* (London, 1938), pp. 476–82.

9 The matter has been studied in detail by J. P. Hyatt in his commentary on Exodus in the *New Century Bible* (London, 1971), pp. 306ff., and to a lesser extent by G. B. Gray in his commentary on Numbers in the *International Critical Commentary* (Edinburgh, 1903), p. 100.

10 A. Oepke, article *'mesitēs'* in *Theological Dictionary of the New Testament*, ed. G. Kittel and G. Friedrich, English translation (Grand Rapids, Michigan, 1972), vol. 4, pp. 612, 613.

11 B. W. Bacon, *Studies in Matthew* (London, 1930).

12 Supporters of the theory include E. P. Blair, *Studies in the Gospel of St Matthew* (London, 1960), pp. 124–37; W. D. Davies, *The Setting of the Sermon on the Mount* (London, 1963), pp. 25–93; R. J. Banks, *Jesus and the Law* (London, 1974), pp. 229–35; R. T. France, *Matthew, Evangelist and Teacher* (London, 1989), pp. 186–8.

13 Matthew 7:28; 11:1; 13:53; 19:1; 26:1.

14 R. Laurentin, *Luc I et II* (Paris, 1964).

15 Laurentin, op. cit., p. 80.

16 J. Jeremias, article 'Moses' in *Theological Dictionary of the New Testament*, English translation (Grand Rapids, Michigan, 1972), vol. 4, p. 873.

6

⊠ *The request for our reconciliation*

Having established that Jesus is the competent mediator for the whole human race, it is now necessary to examine the way in which he interceded on behalf of humanity to secure our reconciliation with the Father.[1] It is a difficult problem because nowhere in the New Testament is the process enacted and described with the same direct simplicity which we see in the past instances where Moses interceded for the sinful Israelites.

As a starting point I would like to reflect for a moment on a detail in the marriage liturgy of the Russian Orthodox Church. When the rings of the bride and bridegroom are blessed, the priest recites a prayer which alludes to all references to rings in the Bible (even that which Judah gave to the supposed prostitute!). The last instance in the prayer is surprising, since it refers to the occasion when God the Father placed a ring on the finger of his son and killed the fatted calf. Clearly this is an allusion to the parable of the prodigal son, who is by implication identified with Christ. Since Jesus had no sins of his own, the identification must be understood as his action in bringing sinful humanity with him on the journey from the foreign land back to the Father.

The context of this task is indicated in the New Testament by using the title 'mediator' for Jesus. It occurs twice in Galatians 3:19–20:

Why then the law? It was added because of transgressions, till the offspring should come to whom the promise had been made; and it was ordained by angels through an intermediary (*mesitou*). Now an intermediary (*mesitēs*) implies more than one; but God is one.

The same technical term occurs also in 1 Timothy 2:5: 'For there is one God, and there is one mediator (*mesitēs*) between God and men, the man Christ Jesus.' The passage in Galatians is complex. St Paul is contrasting the Old and New Covenants, pointing out the superiority of the latter, but in the way he writes he presupposes that his audience has a detailed knowledge of the incident on Sinai when the first one was given. Much of what he says is allusive, and we have to be sensitive to detect the implications. For the purposes of the present enquiry it is interesting to appreciate that Christ's mediation is closely linked with that of Moses. Having stated that Jesus was the mediator, the activity of intercession could be taken for granted at some stage in his career since the matter was so prominent, and so well known, in the life and work of Moses.

At this point it may be useful to introduce a caveat. It is well known that sacrifice can be distorted, when presented as offering compensation to an angry god. What is less obvious is that intercession too can have its caricature. Generations of English schoolchildren have heard the story (and perhaps seen the painting in the House of Commons) of how Queen Philippa interceded with the angry Edward III to spare the burghers of Calais. The intercessory work of Christ was very different from that episode, as will be apparent in this chapter.

At what stage in his career did the work of intercession actually take place? The answer is that it permeated the whole of his public mission, and beyond. The first stage was that of solidarity. In his earthly life Jesus himself went through the stages which sinful individuals should follow, thus giving example in the first instance, as well as asking for their reconciliation. All this he did as a matter of integrity. The very first step was to offer himself to John the Baptist for baptism in the Jordan 'to fulfil all righteousness' (Matthew 3:15). This was a symbolic act not only of example to others, but also of solidarity with the human race. Having become one of us by nature in the incarnation, his presenting himself for baptism was a deliberate act of identification with mankind in our state of collective sinfulness. This was the first stage in the explicit process of leading the human race back to reconciliation with the Father.

The second stage is to be seen in the opening message of his public preaching which was epitomized in the sentence: 'The time is fulfilled, and the Kingdom of God is at hand; repent and believe in the gospel' (Mark 1:15).[2] It is a commonplace of New Testament scholarship that *metanoeite*, which was traditionally translated as 'repent', means more precisely 'turn around', 'be converted', or 'make a new start'. The phrase 'Kingdom of God' has been the subject of many articles and books. For the purposes of this study it is necessary merely to summarize a few relevant concepts in the deep and rich set of ideas which are designated by this famous phrase. Contrary to what was once held, it does not refer to an institution such as a new nation which would perpetuate the ancient state of Israel, nor is it to be identified with the visible Church. It can best be described as a new set of relationships between God and the human race. It presupposes the final revelation of the true God and his purposes to humanity. It implies a state of peace and concord between God and his creatures, in which the will of God is known and consciously pursued by human beings. This situation of harmony between the human race and God commenced in the lifetime of Jesus, and will achieve its fulfilment and perfection only at the end of time with the second coming of Christ. The precise relationship between the Kingdom and the institutional Church on earth is a complex question and lies outside the scope of this book. Clearly the coming and the progress of the Kingdom imply atonement and reconciliation between the sinful human race and the all holy God.

In the task of bringing mankind back to the Father this stage of being invited to 'repent'[3] is essential for a particular reason. In the examples of Moses interceding for the people cited in the previous chapter, the consciousness of fault was already there. It was precisely because the people were aware of having sinned that they turned to Moses to intercede for them and seek reconciliation with God. The situation for Jesus was different. He had not been recognized as a leader or mediator in any sense similar to Moses, and the people had not acknowledged any sinfulness. Nor indeed were they consciously seeking a way back to the God from whom they had become estranged. The first task of his preaching was to elicit from the people the desire for reconciliation. Clearly it would have been pointless for Jesus to have sought forgiveness for a people who were neither aware of, nor repentant for, their sins. With this consideration in mind it is clear that the mediation of Jesus was somewhat different from that of Moses. It can be described as a two-way process of bringing both sides together, urging the people to seek reconciliation and asking the Father to accept them.

Starting with the exhortation to repent, it is reasonable to look upon the public life of Jesus as one long invitation to his hearers to seek reconciliation with God, and to live according to a set of ideals whose observance would make them worthy members of the Kingdom. The explicit requests to his heavenly Father to accept the repentant mortals, and the exhortations to us to return to God, do not occur in a systematic fashion like the logical stages in an educational syllabus. Instead they are scattered throughout his preaching, almost randomly, just as it was in the Old Testament when the prophets recalled Israel to fidelity to the true God.

The Lord's Prayer, not surprisingly, contains the key idea. In the words 'Forgive us our trespasses' (Matthew 6:12) Jesus is deliberately leading the people back to God on the path of repentance, and with them asks the Father for collective forgiveness. Moreover the presence of the request in that archetypal prayer ensured that the idea of reconciliation with the Father would be central to Christian consciousness. In the *Didache* (VIII, 3) we read that the Lord's Prayer was to be recited three times a day. As that document was composed probably in the same period as the writings of the New Testament, one can appreciate how swift was the impact of the Our Father on the infant Church. When Jesus told his hearers that he had come to call not the righteous but the sinners (Matthew 9:13), he did not say exactly what he was calling them to. It is latent in the message, but quite obvious, that he is calling them back to reconciliation with the Father, and by implication it is clear that he is in a position to ensure their acceptance by the Father thanks to his own right of access. The well-known lament: 'Jerusalem, Jerusalem . . .! How often have I longed to gather your children as a hen gathers her children under her wings' (Matthew 23:37), indicates that the only obstacle to the reconciliation is the reluctance of the human party to the deal. The Father's attitude is not in doubt, nor is the competence of Christ. A further example of the non-systematic occurrence of the intercessory theme is to be found in the discourse at the last supper as recorded in the fourth gospel. Jesus prays to his Father using the words: 'I do not pray for these only, but also for those who believe in me through their word, that they may all be one; even as thou, Father, art in me and I in thee' (John 17:20–21). The prayer envisages directly the end result, namely the conscious unity of people united in love, but the implication is that he is asking too for their reconciliation with one another and with the Father, without which the unity would be unattainable.

Having planted the message among the human race sufficiently firmly to ensure its transmission to future generations and other nations, Jesus was in a position to move on to the next stage in his task of seeking and achieving the reconciliation between the human race and God the Father.

This stage is the New Covenant, inaugurated at the Last Supper. The notorious problem as to whether it was a Passover meal or not has been resolved in recent years. Jeremias has provided conclusive reasons for identifying the Last Supper as a Passover meal.[4] The discrepancy between John and the synoptics about the day on which Jesus celebrated the meal can best be accounted for as a theologically motivated literary device by the author of the fourth gospel. In other words he wished his readers to infer that Jesus met his death at the same time as the Passover lambs were being killed in the Temple. According to the literary conventions of the time it was the clearest way of saying that Christ was the true paschal lamb for whom all the others had been prefigurements.

The Covenant is so comprehensive and central to the whole economy of grace that it cannot be simplified to merely one form of contact between man and God. In the complex richness of this institution one strand is that of reconciliation sought and gained by the mediator. The four accounts of the Last Supper can be grouped into two pairs.[5] Luke and Paul bear the marks of more theological elaboration than Mark or Matthew. In the latter pair Matthew has signs of Greek overtones to clarify Mark's simpler Semitic wording. The reliability and authenticity of the accounts cannot reasonably be doubted. On this matter I will quote Jeremias:

We have every reason to conclude that the common core of the tradition of the account of the Lord's supper – what Jesus said at the Last Supper – is preserved to us in an essentially reliable form.[6]

As recorded in Mark the exact words of the enactment are:

And he took a cup and when he had given thanks he gave it to them, and they all drank of it. And he said to them 'This is my blood of the [new] covenant which is poured out for many.' (Mark 14:23–24)

The word 'new' in the foregoing quotation is of questionable authenticity, being absent from some of the oldest manuscripts, but it does not alter the argument materially. The wording of this incident indicates that Jesus and the evangelist wished to stress the resemblance to the covenant at Sinai, with Moses as the mediator, as recorded in Exodus 24:8.

At this stage it is necessary to say a brief word about the notion of covenant and its theological significance. As is well known, the technical term in Hebrew (translated into Greek for the Septuagint, and taken thence into the New Testament) is the ordinary profane word for a contract of any kind. It could be used for sale and purchase, for a marriage, or for political alliances. The precise model which served the ancient Israelites for their religious covenant has been much debated, but need not detain us here. By the time of Jesus it had acquired a theological significance in its own right. Although derived from the simple concept of a contract, it is important to remember, from the theological point of view, that it was not confined to an agreement between two equal parties. As a tool for the theologians this is important, since it denotes the institutionalizing of relations between God and human beings, thanks to which the latter can count on favours from God. From the standpoint of human psychology this sense of security is important, and in the covenant relationship it is secured without any claim to laying upon God obligations of justice which he might seem to owe to his creatures.

At its very core the Covenant implies concord and reconciliation between God and man, and that is why I stress its importance at this stage in tracing the intercessory role of Jesus in seeking to reunite the human race with the Father. Christ's inauguration of the New Covenant was one stage in the intercessory process.

In the New Testament the word 'covenant' occurs 26 times and sixteen of these instances are allusions to the former covenant of Sinai. I mention this fact because it is important to remember how closely the New and Old Covenants are related. In the letters of St Paul the word occurs only half-a-dozen times but the idea is present more pervasively than that number would suggest.[7] His explanation of the relationship between the two covenants is that the New has perfected the Old, and not invalidated it. The Letter to the Hebrews takes a somewhat different view, describing the Old Covenant as being quite simply obsolete (Hebrews 8:13). Both schools of thought agree that Jesus is the mediator (cf. Hebrews 9:15 etc.).

In their presentation of the New Covenant it is clear that the writers of the New Testament were more influenced by Isaiah and Jeremiah than by the accounts of the covenant in the Pentateuch. As time passed the prophets looked ahead to the inauguration of another covenant which would surpass the Mosaic one, and in which the keynote would be the forgiveness of sins. In Hebrews 8:8–12 we read a verbatim quotation from Jeremiah on this very matter. The passage in the original prophecy of Jeremiah is as follows:

Behold the days are coming, says the Lord, when I will make a new covenant with the house of Israel and the house of Judah, not like the covenant which I made with their fathers when I took them by the hand to bring them out of the land of Egypt, my covenant which they broke, though I was their husband, says the Lord. But this is the covenant which I will make with the house of Israel after those days, says the Lord: I will put my law within them, and I will write it upon their hearts; and I will be their God and they shall be my people. And no longer shall each man teach his neighbour and his brother saying 'Know the Lord', for they shall all know me, from the least of them to the greatest, says the Lord; for I will forgive their iniquity, and I will remember their sin no more. (Jeremiah 31:31–34)

It has been suggested that the words about the new covenant were inserted into Jeremiah by the deuteronomistic school who edited the prophet's speeches. For the present study it is immaterial at what stage the concept entered the text. By the time of Jesus those words had stood in the text of Jeremiah for centuries, and it was that form of the text which influenced the thinking of his contemporaries.

It is difficult to overestimate the importance of this passage in Jeremiah, since it deals with so much which is central to Christian theology. As far as the present book is concerned, I wish to emphasize the last sentence of the quotation, where reconciliation is spoken of, since it must influence our understanding of the Christian covenant.

The same message of repentance and turning from sin is to be seen in another prophecy concerning the new covenant, which is in the third part of Isaiah.

So they shall fear the name of the Lord . . . and he will come to Zion as a redeemer to those in Jacob who turn from transgressions, says the Lord. And as for me this is my covenant with them, says the Lord: my spirit which is upon you, and my words which I have put into your mouth, shall not depart out of your mouth, or out of the mouth of your children, or out of the mouth of your children's children, says the Lord, from this time forth and for evermore. (Isaiah 59:19–21)

It is my contention that the New Covenant inaugurated at the Last Supper is to be understood as an act of reconciliation between the human race and God. (There is much more in it besides this, but for the purposes of this book I wish to confine my attention to that one aspect.)

There are two other considerations which deserve careful reflection. Firstly the matter of sacrifice: both the Sinai covenant and that of Jesus were accompanied by sacrifices, but in both cases the institution itself (the covenant) is distinct, and to some extent separate, from the sacrifice which accompanies it. I feel that it is necessary to stress this point because so many writers have assumed either that the liberation from sin is achieved only by the sacrifice, or that the covenant is indistinguishable from the attendant sacrifice.

The second consideration is even more important. Whereas the Sinai covenant was initiated by God, it would seem that the New Covenant was actually initiated by Jesus. He chose the time, place and circumstances of the inauguration. It seems clear, at least by implication, that he felt competent to do so. And it is not unreasonable to assume that in his consciousness of his mission as Messiah he was competent to undertake this momentous action, which had been foretold by the prophets. If it seems strange to emphasize that Jesus initiated the covenant, it is helpful to reflect that other activities of his messianic mission were not dictated to him by the Father as if he were devoid of initiative. In such matters as his preaching, miracles, selection and training of his disciples, Jesus took the initiative and acted on his own responsibility, knowing of course that his activity was in accord with the will of the Father. It is my contention that in the inauguration of the New Covenant he exercised a similar degree of autonomy in what was perhaps the most significant step in his asking for reconciliation on behalf of humanity.

Gathering together the ideas of the preceding pages, I suggest that the institution of the New Covenant, within which the forgiveness of sins was an integral part, was a substantial stage in Jesus' work of intercession. In other words, it was equivalent to asking for the forgiveness of the whole human race.[8] The fact that it was expressed in words different from those employed in similar instances in the career of Moses need not surprise us. The circumstances were totally different. Moses prayed for pardon after a particular sin of a particular group. Jesus was seeking atonement for all the sins of the whole human race. This being the case, the request had to be given a degree of permanence, hence its being enshrined in covenant form. Just how far the factor of permanence entered into the process is important, and I will return to it later in the chapter.

In the light of what I have said about the covenant at the Last Supper, I feel that it is reasonable to look upon the crucifixion as being an act of intercession, in addition to its many other aspects. As far as Jesus was concerned, his enduring of suffering was an act of witness in fidelity to his teaching, which he would not compromise, even to save his own life. That teaching had been a total programme of bringing the human race into a harmonious relationship with God the Father. He had encouraged people to adopt a simple trust in God with no reliance on substitutes like the Law, or Jewish ancestry. This was part of what aroused hostility in his enemies, and for which they killed him. His intercession on behalf of the human race consisted in actions, teaching and witness in addition to the specific requests for reconciliation.

At various places in this book I have spoken of intercession. The time has come to examine the concept more closely in the context of those passages in the New Testament where the word is employed. The Greek word for intercession, *tugchanō*, underwent a complex evolution.[9] In secular Greek usage it meant 'hit' as of an arrow reaching its target. In that sense the Septuagint used the word to translate the Hebrew *matsa*, as in Deuteronomy 19:5, where the axe head flies off and hits a bystander. In Greek the word developed into the senses of 'happen', 'encounter', and later 'complain' or 'petition'. In this latter sense it could conveniently be used to translate various aspects of prayer, as in Daniel 6:13, where Daniel prays to God, and also in Wisdom 8:21, 'I entreated the Lord'. In the New Testament it is used twice in the sense of approaching someone with a complaint, and four times in the restricted sense of intercession.[10]

For the purposes of this study the occurrence in Romans 8:34 is of exceptional importance. St Paul is speaking of the liberation of mankind from sin, in the imagery of a law court:

Who shall bring any charge against God's elect? It is God who justifies; who is to condemn? Is it Christ Jesus who died, yes, who was raised from the dead, who is at the right hand of God who indeed intercedes for us?

The context of this passage is the rescue of the human race from all the consequences of sin, and the eventual reward of the elect in heaven. The three elements of Christ's liberating work are referred to, namely the death and resurrection together with his role as intercessor. It would be artificial to separate these three too radically, but it is worth noting that in this passage the death and resurrection are mentioned as plain occurrences in his life's journey, whereas the truly causal part of the liberating process is designated as the intercessory role with the Father. The imagery of being at the right hand is common in the Bible, and in subsequent credal statements. It denotes basic equality with the Father and implies divinity. As I showed in a previous chapter, this fact of his being divine was an essential element in Jesus' competence to be the spokesman for the human race. It does no violence to the text to understand St Paul's thought as ascribing to the intercession of Jesus the causal role in securing the atonement for humanity. The standard commentaries agree on this.[11]

The aspect of permanence, and therefore timelessness, is implied because the activity of intercession takes place after the resurrection, when Jesus is in glory with the Father. This important facet of the intercession taking place in eternity is indicated more clearly in the Letter to the Hebrews.[12]

According to the author of Hebrews, the nature of Jesus' intercession is determined by the fact that his priesthood is permanent.[13] This is expressed most forcibly in Hebrews 7:23–24: 'The former priests were many in number, because they were prevented by death from continuing in office; but he holds his priesthood permanently, because he continues for ever.' As is well known, this permanence and the very nature of Jesus' priesthood derive directly from the incarnation. Being the perfect union of human and divine in one person, Jesus had fulfilled completely the requirements for a priest, namely to be a satisfactory representative of the human race in relation to God.

Having declared that Jesus' priestly office is permanent, the writer then goes on to spell out explicitly what this means for his priestly function: 'Consequently he is able for all time to save those who draw near to God through him, since he is always alive to make intercession for them' (Hebrews 7:25). It is virtually impossible to state the matter more clearly, and any comment is in danger of obscuring the lucid statement of the inspired text. There is no question of presenting a ransom or placating an angry deity. The role of Christ is quite simply to ask for forgiveness.

I have emphasized the importance of this particular passage in Hebrews because it encompasses the difficult problem of eternity. If the redemptive work of Jesus is to benefit those who live and died both before and after the period of his earthly life, then his act of liberation must cross over the boundary from the world of time and become effective in the realm of eternity. It is perhaps superfluous to bear in mind that eternity is not to be conceived of as if it were 'a long time'. It is totally different from time. This philosophical concept was scarcely analysed by the writers of the New Testament, and was elaborated after the New Testament epoch by Greek-speaking theologians in the light of Hellenistic philosophy. This passage in Hebrews is the closest that we find in the New Testament to a treatise on time and eternity. Without pursuing the matter in further detail, one can say that to have situated the intercession of Christ in this perspective ensures that it can cope with the problems which had been raised in connection with the salvation of those who lived before Christ came to earth.

Basically the same idea is to be found also in Hebrews 9:24: 'For Christ has entered, not into a sanctuary made with hands, a copy of the true one, but into heaven itself, now to appear in the presence of God on our behalf.' This sentence fits into the writer's comparison of Christ's sacrifice with that in the liturgy of the Day of Atonement. The author alludes to the annual Jewish festival whose purpose was the request for the collective forgiveness of the sins committed by the whole people. Two goats were selected, one was killed and the other driven out into the wilderness, symbolically taking away with it the sins of the nation. Moreover, to stress the importance of the festival, it was the only occasion in the course of the year when the high priest went into the inner sanctuary, the Holy of Holies. The author of Hebrews envisages that entry as a pale reflection of the true sanctuary which is heaven, and Jesus' entry there after the resurrection. That was without any ambiguity the coming into the presence of God the Father, for which the annual ceremony in the Temple in Jerusalem was merely a symbolic representation.

The actual entry into the divine presence is designated by the technical word *emphanizō* whose fundamental meaning is 'make visible' or 'manifest'. In the New Testament it usually carries the meaning of making an official report, or signifying a request.[14] In the present instance the context makes it clear that Christ is not making a request to the Father on behalf of himself, but for sinful human beings. It is parallel to Hebrews 7:25 and denotes the act of intercession.[15]

Various of the Fathers duly record the fact of Christ's intercession, but without special emphasis, presumably because in their cultural perspectives it would have been regarded as a normal activity for the mediator, requiring no special explanation, unlike the crucifixion. In their commentaries and homilies on Romans and Hebrews one can read their observations on the activity as they comment on the key texts of Romans 8:34 and Hebrews 7:25. Of the surviving commentaries on Romans, the intercessory work of Christ is duly noted by Origen, Chrysostom, Theodoret of Cyrrhus and Ambrosiaster.[16] Augustine commented on Romans but not on this passage.[17] There are notably fewer patristic commentaries on Hebrews, perhaps because of the doubts, in the early centuries, about its canonicity. Chrysostom and Theodoret of Cyrrhus acknowledge Christ's intercession in the context of 7:25.[18] Their principal preoccupation in Christ's intercession was their insistence that he did it in virtue of his human nature. This was doubtless because of the trinitarian and christological controversies which were raging in their lifetimes. Origen wrote a commentary on Hebrews but its surviving fragments do not cover the key texts about intercession. The same fate befell the commentaries on Romans of both Diodore of Tarsus and Theodore of Mopsuestia, and also the latter's commentary on Hebrews. Fragments gathered from the catenae and other sources have not brought to light the passages relevant to the key texts which we are examining.[19] It is significant that the Fathers of the Eastern Church have studied the question of intercession far more frequently than their confrères in the West, where the concept of satisfaction was steadily gaining ground.

One other passage in Hebrews has sometimes been understood as a prayer of Christ for the forgiveness of humanity's sins, namely Hebrews 5:7, where we read: 'In the days of his flesh, Jesus offered up prayers and supplications, with loud cries and tears, to him who was able to save him from death, and he was heard for his godly fear.' The phrase 'prayers and supplications' is more precise than its form would suggest to a modern reader. In antiquity it was a technical expression in use from the third century BC and denoted the addressing of a petition to the emperor or some other important functionary. It has been suggested that in this instance it should be understood as the intercessory prayer of Jesus on behalf of the human race.[20] The suggestion has attracted little support, although it seems to have had Chrysostom and Theophylact as its precursors in antiquity. It is more satisfactory to understand it as Christ's prayer to be delivered from the pains of death, which was answered in a superlative form in his resurrection.[21]

I have made the claim that Christ secured the atonement for the human race basically by intercession, in other words asking for our reconciliation with God. I am well aware that this activity features far less frequently in the pages of the New Testament than does the notion of an expiatory death.

This can be accounted for quite simply. Whereas the notion of the Messiah making intercession for sins would present no difficulty for the first Christians, who had grown up in Judaism, the violent execution of the Messiah was an almost unsupportable problem. Very quickly they came to understand it in the context of sacrifice, and would have used every opportunity to emphasize its positive significance, lest they or their interlocutors should be overwhelmed by the apparently unmitigated disaster. The same anomaly of a relatively meagre allocation of space applies to another aspect of the atonement, namely the resurrection. Until quite recently theologians and biblical scholars scarcely alluded to its place in the process of liberating mankind from sin, because Christian theology was so preoccupied with the crucifixion. Having understood the degrading death of Jesus in a positive and creative way, the early Christians gave great prominence to it in their writings. This, I think, accounts for the fact that the intercession of Christ, which is presented formally in the New Testament, does not receive as much space there as the crucifixion does. The precise relationship between the crucifixion, the resurrection and the intercessory activity of Jesus must be left to Chapter 8, where the reader will be in a position to appreciate a balanced view of this delicate question.

By way of summary of the material in this chapter, I wish to repeat the all-important fact that the sins of the human race were forgiven, and we were reconciled with the Father thanks to the simple fact that Jesus requested just this. The signs that his intercession had been successful were the resurrection and the bestowal of the Holy Spirit. Once this basic reconciliation had been established in principle, it remains for individuals to respond to the offers of grace, and to take up in their own lives the pattern of behaviour which is in accord with the will of God.

NOTES

1 This field has been almost totally neglected by modern writers. I know of only one author who touches on the matter: R. S. Wallace, *The Atoning Death of Christ* (Westchester, Illinois, 1981), devotes two paragraphs to it in passing (p. 124), citing Hooker's *Laws*, V, 51.

2 The same proclamation is recorded with only minor variations in Matthew 4:17.

3 I will continue to use the word 'repent' since, although it is not a totally satisfactory translation of the Greek, it has been consecrated by long usage, and there is no other single word with which to replace it in practice.

4 J. Jeremias, *The Eucharistic Words of Jesus* (English translation of the revised edition of 1964; London, 1966), pp. 41–61.

5 Recorded also with only minor variations in Matthew 26:22–29; Luke 22:15–20; 1 Corinthians 11:23–25.

6 Jeremias, op. cit., p. 203.

7 Romans 11:27; 1 Corinthians 11:25; 2 Corinthians 3:6, 14; Galatians 3:17.

8 The words 'for many' in Matthew 26:28 are the literal translation of a well-known Semitism which is equivalent to 'all people'.

9 Otto Bauernfeind, article *'tugchanō'* in *Theological Dictionary of the New Testament*, ed. G. Kittel and G. Friedrich, English translation (Grand Rapids, Michigan, 1972), vol. 8. pp. 238–43; A. Gonzalez, article 'Prière' in *Dictionnaire de la Bible* (Supplement), vol. 8 (Paris, 1972), col. 596.

10 Romans 8:26, 27, 34; Hebrews 7:25.

11 C. H. Dodd, *The Epistle of St Paul to the Romans* (London, 1954), p. 145; H. Schlier, *Der Römerbrief* (Freiburg, 1979), p. 278; E. Käsemann, *Commentary on Romans*, English translation (London, 1980), p. 248.

12 For what follows I am indebted principally to the commentary of C. Spicq, *Epître aux Hébreux*, vol. 2 (Paris, 1953), pp. 197ff.

13 Hebrews 7:11–24, 28; 9:11.

14 Acts 23:15, 22; 25:15.

15 Spicq, op. cit., p. 267.

16 Origen: PG 14, 1130; Chrysostom: PG 60, 543; Theodoret of Cyrrhus: PG 82, 143; Ambrosiaster: PL 17, 135.

17 Augustine: CSEL, vol. 84, p. 31.

18 Chrysostom: PG 63, 105; Theodoret of Cyrrhus: PG 82, 731.

19 Origen: PG 14, 1307; Diodore of Tarsus and Theodore of Mopsuestia in K. Staab, *Pauluskommentare aus der griechischen Kirche* (Münster, 1933), pp. 96, 141, 208.
20 A. Vitti, article in *Verbum Domini* (1934), pp. 86–92, 108–12.
21 Spicq, op. cit., p. 117.

7

⊠ *The inevitable crucifixion*

Having emphasized the central role of intercession in Christ's work of liberation, it is now important to face up to some difficult questions about his death. Was it avoidable or inevitable? Was it necessary? And if so, whence did the necessity arise? From the decree of the Father? Did he require it as the price of reconciliation, as has so often been suggested?

In the light of what I have stated in the preceding chapters I hope that it is clear that the death of Jesus was not demanded by God as the precondition for the atonement. Once that point has been established, the identification of the real cause of his execution is somewhat harder. The solution is best sought by tracing in the gospels the stages in the mounting opposition to Jesus, which culminated in his crucifixion.[1]

At first sight it is difficult to see why he should have met with a violent death. He did not provoke confrontation with the authorities. Throughout his public career he refused to conform to popular expectations of a political Messiah, modelled on the image of a warrior king like David, or more recently like Judas Maccabeus, who within recent memory had led a nationalist uprising against the Seleucid oppressors. The power of such expectations can be seen by the enthusiasm with which the nation took up the rebellion, merely one generation after Jesus, which led to the destruction of Jerusalem by Titus and Vespasian in AD 70. Two generations after that, Bar Kochba was able to generate similar fervour in his uprising, which ended in the destruction of the nation in 135.

On the other hand Jesus was not the preacher of a purely moral crusade, like John the Baptist,[2] and herein lies the subtlety of his mission and the nature of the opposition which it provoked.

Although Jesus kept clear of plain politics, his preaching of the Kingdom of God implied a profound criticism of the existing religious and political establishments, and the implications were probably perceived at least dimly by the authorities from the start. Hence the sense of danger even early in his preaching career, because opposition was there from the start.[3] After the arrest of John the Baptist Jesus felt it necessary to withdraw to Galilee (Matthew 4:12).

Several times in the course of his teaching he predicted his own death. Three such warnings are preserved in the synoptics,[4] but there may well have been more.

What exactly was the nature of the latent opposition between Jesus and the authorities? To elucidate this it will be necessary to glance briefly at the religious and secular structures which held sway at that epoch. Since the time of Herod the Great in the last century BC, the Jews had lost their political independence. Although Herod and his sons were allowed to retain titles like king or tetrarch, they were puppet rulers and exercised only as much power as the Romans would allow them. Foreign policy, war and peace, taxation and the preservation of public order were in the hands of the Romans, as was the death penalty. As with all their colonies, the Romans were tolerant of local customs and religions. They operated by what would now be called the principle of subsidiarity. Provided that they presented no threat to Roman suzerainty the local political leaders and the ruling class had a fairly comfortable time, and it suited the occupying power to let the Jewish leaders carry on with the pedestrian business of everyday life. Since religion and secular affairs were not separate as in the modern world, the same limited autonomy was granted to the religious leaders as well. Among the Jews this was of particular significance. Since the return from the Babylonian exile in the sixth century BC the Jewish nation had been virtually a theocracy under the leadership of the high priest, who in turn had been controlled by various political masters, firstly in the Persian empire and latterly under the Romans. He and the senior priests, together with their party the Sadducees, continued to enjoy great privileges and respect among the people.

The other religious party, the Pharisees, conducted a different way of life. They had woven round themselves a web of religious observances which was so complex, and yet so satisfying in its observance, that they could ignore secular politics, and the power which the Romans exercised over their nation seems to have had little impact on their day-to-day concerns.

As a result of this delicate balance of interests, both the Romans and the Jewish leaders were happy that things should carry on as before, undisturbed. Clearly the Romans would be the more sensitive to any political subversion, and they knew by experience that manifestations of religious enthusiasm could quickly be translated into political unrest, and violent revolution. The uprisings of Theudas and Judas the Galilean, mentioned in Acts, were of this kind, as were similar disturbances recorded by Josephus.[5]

Of the various elements in the hostility between Jesus and the Palestinian establishment, the opposition of the Pharisees is the most amply documented in the gospels. This is probably because their religious stance presented the most stubborn obstacle to the message of Jesus. Unlike the Sadducees, whose obvious worldliness was plain for all to see, the Pharisees presented an apparently edifying example of religious zeal. In one sense it was edifying because of the effort entailed in the observance of literally hundreds of rules for the sanctification of every detail of daily life. Although they were inspired by the Bible, all the regulations were basically man-made, and the integral observance of this complex code distracted their practitioners from the real moral issues of justice and the love of God. Psychologically too they felt satisfied, and as such they proved to be more impenetrable to the message of Jesus than the sinners who, having no illusions about their own virtue, were open to the influence of his gospel.

The opposition between the stance of the Pharisees and the teaching of Jesus is summarized by St Matthew in the long speech in chapter 23. Clearly this is an artificial grouping of sayings, and it is clear from other indications in the synoptics that the friction was constant. The opening section indicates the fundamental flaw in their spirituality, namely that it was made up of humanly devised regulations being passed off as the will of God. In all fairness to them, one ought to bear in mind that Christians of later ages have done almost the same thing with the rules of Churches or religious orders. The integral observance of such sets of regulations can give a profound sense of security, but it can also have debilitating effects on people's real spiritual maturity, inhibiting it in countless ways. To both classes of enthusiasts, Jewish or Christian, the words of Jesus are a sober warning: 'The scribes and the pharisees sit on Moses' seat . . . they bind heavy burdens, hard to bear, and lay them on men's shoulders' (Matthew 23:2, 4). The man-made as opposed to divine origin of the regulations is emphasized also in Mark's gospel:

Now when the pharisees gathered together to him, with some of the scribes, who had come from Jerusalem, they saw that some of his disciples ate with hands defiled, that is, unwashed. (For the pharisees, and all the Jews, do not eat unless they wash their hands, observing the tradition of the elders; and when they come from the market place they do not eat unless they purify themselves; and there are many other traditions which they observe, the washing of cups and pots and vessels of bronze.) And the pharisees and the scribes asked him, 'Why do your disciples not live according to the tradition of the elders, but eat with hands defiled?' (Mark 7:1–5)

The really harmful effects of keeping the human regulations are emphasized in Matthew, where the convenient observance of the man-made duty was taken as an excuse to opt out of the God-given responsibility of caring for aged parents, on a technicality of having put the money at the disposal of the Temple:

The pharisees and scribes came to Jesus from Jerusalem and said, 'Why do your disciples transgress the tradition of the elders? For they do not wash their hands when they eat.' He answered them 'And why do you transgress the commandment of God for the sake of your tradition? For God commanded "Honour your father and your mother", and "he who speaks ill of father or mother let him surely die." But you say, "If any one tells his father or mother, What you would have gained from me is given to God, he need not honour his father." So for the sake of your tradition you have made void the word of God.' (Matthew 15:1–6)

Part of the satisfaction which the Pharisees derived from their religious observances was the amount of social privilege which these conferred on them among the ordinary people. This too was condemned by Jesus:

They do all their deeds to be seen by men; for they make their phylacteries broad and their fringes long, and they love the places of honour at feasts and the best seats in the synagogues, and salutations in the market places, and being called rabbi by men. But you are not to be called rabbi, for you have one teacher, and you are all brethren. And call no man your father on earth, for you have one Father who is in heaven. Neither be called masters for you have one master, the Christ. (Matthew 23:5–10)

The observance of their code of rules gave the Pharisees prestige in the eyes of their co-religionists, and gave psychological satisfaction to themselves for completing so difficult a programme.

Both these factors would have kept them from recognizing the real moral issues which the authentic service of God demanded. A secular prophet of a later age would surely have discerned there the opiate of the people. Jesus unmasked it directly and accused them in words which have become proverbial in the English language:

Woe to you scribes and pharisees, hypocrites! for you tithe mint and dill and cummin, and have neglected the weightier matters of the law, justice, and mercy and faith; these you ought to have done without neglecting the others. You blind guides, straining out a gnat and swallowing a camel! (Matthew 23:23–24)

One can detect in these bitter tirades against the Pharisees the frustration which Jesus must have felt because they opposed the gospel of the Kingdom by what they considered to be the authentic religion of Moses. The irony could not have been more cruel. In this way their hostility to Jesus was basically the same as the opposition to the ancient prophets by the priests and the establishment of their day. Perhaps this explains the bitterness which one sees in the last section of that long speech:

Woe to you scribes and pharisees, hypocrites! for you build the tombs of the prophets and adorn the monuments of the righteous, saying, 'If we had lived in the days of our fathers, we would not have taken part with them in shedding the blood of the prophets.' Thus you witness against yourselves, that you are sons of those who murdered the prophets. Fill up then the measure of your fathers. You serpents, you brood of vipers, how are you to escape from the sentence of hell? Therefore I send you prophets and wise men and scribes, some of whom you will kill and crucify, and some you will scourge in your synagogues and persecute from town to town, that upon you may come all the righteous blood shed on earth, from the blood of innocent Abel to the blood of Zechariah the son of Barachiah, whom you murdered between the sanctuary and the altar. Truly I say to you, all this will come upon this generation. (Matthew 23:29–36)

Although one cannot be certain about the chronology of the public life of Jesus, it seems that his opponents began to plan his downfall quite early. After the account of a healing miracle on the sabbath, which was a technical infringement of the Law, we read that the Pharisees started planning with the party of Herod about silencing Jesus: 'The pharisees went out and immediately held counsel with the Herodians against him, how to destroy him' (Mark 3:6). The implication is that they wanted to put him to death, which would have required the sanction of the Roman authorities. This was probably the motive behind the tricky question by which they sought to entrap him into urging the non-payment of taxes, and which earned the famous reply to 'render to Caesar the things that are Caesar's'. At the trial of Jesus that incident was remembered in the endeavour to make against him the case of political subversion: 'We found this man perverting our nation, and forbidding us to give tribute to Caesar, and saying that he himself is Christ, a king' (Luke 23:2).

In addition to the hostility of the Pharisees and the party of Herod, it seems clear that Jesus incurred the enmity of the high priests as well. At the psychological level there is a striking parallel between the reception of Jesus' preaching and that of John Wesley seventeen centuries later. After Wesley's definitive conversion in 1738 he preached in a number of London churches, and was systematically excluded from them thereafter. In the following year John Wesley and his brother Charles started preaching in Bristol and the surrounding country. There too opposition was strong. Dr Butler, the bishop of Bristol, wrote to him:

Sir, pretending to extraordinary revelations and gifts of the Holy Ghost is a horrid thing; yes, Sir, it is a very horrid thing. Sir, you have no business here; you are not commissioned to preach in this diocese: therefore I advise you to go hence.

Opposition, hostility and resentment followed the early Methodists wherever they went. The causes are not difficult to identify. John Wesley and his followers preached the message of the gospel without compromise, and were resented by the established clergy who had made all too many compromises with the world in the security of their comfortable lives. Even if they were not rich, they had no financial hazards, and a respected place in society. The last thing that they wanted was a radical return to the uncompromising demands of the gospel. The situation between Jesus and the high priests was much the same.

The most dramatic incident in the tension between Jesus and those who controlled the Temple was the expulsion of the buyers and sellers, which is recorded in all four gospels (Matthew 21:12–13; Mark 11:15–17; Luke 19:45–46; John 2:14–20). The fact that the synoptics place it at the very end of his public ministry, whereas John relates it at the start, presents problems of its own. However these need not detain us here, since it is the political impact of the incident which is relevant to the present investigation. The dramatic expulsion of the traders has been interpreted in

somewhat different ways. Traditionally most Christian commentators have viewed it as a symbolic gesture, similar to those of the
Old Testament prophets, which they acted out when a message of
particular importance had to be conveyed to the people. Quite
recently a Jewish scholar has invested the incident with much
greater significance.[6] According to Chilton the incident was
something like a declaration of war, since it was a way of denying,
explicitly, the legitimacy of the sacrifices which were being offered
there. At the risk of some measure of oversimplification his
arguments can be summarized as relying on Hillel and Zechariah.
According to the school of Hillel the animals which were to be
sacrificed had to be the actual possession of the offerers, and
purchase on site was not good enough. According to Zechariah no
trader was to be allowed into the Temple. Admittedly Zechariah
14:21 states explicitly that 'there shall no longer be a trader in the
house of the Lord on that day'. It may be argued that the prophecy
has in mind the eschatological Day of the Lord, and not the
historical era in which Jesus lived. On the other hand, Jesus may
well have considered that his messianic mission was just the
occasion which Zechariah had in mind. Whatever may be the
outcome of that delicate task of interpreting the exact significance
of the incident, its practical impact must have been to provoke the
hostility of the high priests.

In the main, the opposition from this section of the establishment is documented principally in the fourth gospel, and therein
lies its problem for the historian. Because that gospel was written
probably two generations after the events which it records, and
since it bears clear signs of comprehensive theological editing, it is
difficult to decide in any particular case whether or not we have the
authentic words of the speakers as reported. The problem is well
known to New Testament scholars, and its intricacies need not
detain us here. What is clear is that at the trial of Jesus the high
priestly party was openly seeking his execution. This degree of
animosity could not have arisen suddenly, but it is consistent with
the indications of their hostility throughout his public life, as
recorded in the gospels, and particularly in St John.

Jesus' decision to go up to Jerusalem for the festival of
Tabernacles is presented in the context of his awareness of the
intention of his enemies to bring about his death. The events are
recorded in chapter 7 of St John in an atmosphere of mounting
tension and drama. The chapter opens with the words: 'After this

Jesus went about in Galilee; he would not go about in Judea, because the Jews sought to kill him. Now the Jews' feast of Tabernacles was at hand' (John 7:1–2). Eventually Jesus did go up to Jerusalem for the festival and in the middle of it he broke his silence and caused surprise by speaking openly. St John takes up the narrative:

Some of the people of Jerusalem therefore said, 'Is not this the man whom they seek to kill? And there he is, speaking openly, and they say nothing to him! Can it be that the authorities really know that this is the Christ?' . . . So they sought to arrest him but no one laid hands on him, because his hour had not yet come. Yet many of the people believed in him; they said, 'When the Christ appears, will he do more signs than this man has done?' The pharisees heard the crowd thus muttering about him, and the chief priests and the pharisees sent officers to arrest him. Jesus said 'I shall be with you a little longer and then I go to him who sent me' . . . When they heard these words some of the people said, 'This is really the prophet.' Others said 'This is the Christ' . . . So there was a division among the people over him. Some of them wanted to arrest him, but no one laid hands on him. The officers went back to the chief priests and the pharisees, who said to them 'Why did you not bring him?' The officers answered 'No man ever spoke like this man!' (John 7:25–26, 30–33, 40–41, 43–46).

It is in the fourth gospel that we read the account of the raising to life of Lazarus. The only parts of the narrative which concern us here are the initial fears of the disciples, the reaction of the chief priests, and the part which this incident played in the final stages of the drama which culminated in the crucifixion. Although the disciples frequently failed to understand the meaning of Jesus, on this occasion they perceived clearly the perils which were closing in on the Master. When they realized that Jesus intended to go into Judaea to the house of Lazarus they exclaimed: 'Rabbi, the Jews were but now seeking to stone you, and are you going there again?' (John 11:8). When it was clear that Jesus was determined to go there they decided to stick with him: 'Thomas, called the Twin, said to his fellow disciples, "Let us also go, that we may die with him"' (John 11:16). As I stated earlier, it is not possible to be certain about the authenticity of every word which is attributed to the various speakers in the narrative, but the conclusion of the incident is thoroughly consistent with the mounting opposition to Jesus on the part of the authorities. After St John's account of the raising of Lazarus we read of their reaction:

The chief priests and the pharisees gathered the council and said, 'What are we to do? For this man performs many signs. If we let him go on thus, everyone will believe in him, and the Romans will come and destroy both our holy place and our nation.' (John 11:47–48)

That sentence is an ironic comment on mixed motives. The holy place was of course the Temple, and since it was the only place in which sacrifice was permitted under Jewish law, one can sympathize with a certain measure of righteous anxiety. Reading between the lines though, one detects also the well-founded fear about the termination of the comfortable and privileged life style of the priests and the Pharisees, if the Romans intervened violently. The Pharisees feared the end of a way of life in which they enjoyed great prestige, and the priests would also lose wealth and political influence. As with so many similar situations in history, it was not just a question of religious purity, but other sociological factors were operating too.[7] The evangelist's comment at the end of that meeting is succinct and ominous: 'So from that day on they took counsel how to put him to death' (John 11:53).

Their intentions appear to have been common knowledge, probably because they were on the look-out for informers and information about Jesus' movements. The evangelist remarks: 'Jesus no longer went about openly among the Jews' (John 11:54), and the chapter ends with the statement that the authorities were actively seeking to arrest him: 'The chief priests and the pharisees had given orders that if anyone knew where he was, he should let them know, so that they might arrest him' (John 11:57).

Thus did the drama proceed ineluctably towards its tragic climax, wherein the prophet would not compromise his integrity, and where his compromised opponents did everything in their power to be rid of so unsettling an influence to their complacent lifestyle.

In the last analysis it is clear that it was not the will of the Heavenly Father which had required the death of Jesus, but the hostility of his earthly opponents. It is important to appreciate the significance of this, in view of the erstwhile influence of the ransom and satisfaction theories of the atonement.

It is now possible to give a clear answer to the question which was asked at the beginning of the book, which was: 'Why did Jesus have to die on the cross?' The answer is now plain for us to see. The answer is very simple: 'It was the hostility of his enemies which brought about his death.' Spelling it out a little more explicitly, we can say that the uncompromising purity of Jesus' teaching and the integrity of his way of life presented a serious threat to the formalism of the religious observance of both the wealthy and privileged Sadducees and the passionately earnest Pharisees. Neither party could accommodate the radical programme presented in his preaching about the Kingdom of Heaven, and confrontation was inevitable. The situation has been expressed succinctly by the liberation theologian Segundo in these words: 'I have indicated the importance Jesus placed on dismantling the ideological religious apparatus that served, however unwittingly, to oppress the multitude in Israel.'[8]

The collusion of both Roman and Jewish authorities can be seen in the complex process of the trial of Jesus, first of all before the Sanhedrin and finally before Pilate. In the Jewish court he was condemned on the technicality of alleged blasphemy, but to secure the death sentence at the hands of the Romans he had to be accused of political agitation. Whether Pilate was convinced or not is hard to say, and equally hard to determine is whether the Romans considered him to be a member of the guerrilla movement, the Zealots.[9] However it is beyond doubt that he was executed by crucifixion. The Jewish punishment for a purely religious crime of blasphemy would have been death by stoning, as was the case with Stephen. Crucifixion was used by the Romans for ordinary criminals and for political subversives.[10] No one would seriously suggest that he was perceived as a criminal; so we can conclude safely that the Romans condemned him for political subversion.

Behind these legal manoeuvres and sociological influences lies a profound psychological factor. As with many other people of integrity in the course of history, Jesus' own single-mindedness posed a threat to the compromises and vested interests of his contemporaries. Similar psychological factors can be seen to have operated in the violent deaths of people like Thomas Becket, who was killed at the instigation of King Henry II, and Joan of Arc. Her case is of singular interest in view of the alliance of Church and State similar to the collusion between religion and politics in the condemnation of Jesus. She was captured as a prisoner of war by the English, but the Church authorities were prevailed upon to condemn her as a witch, in the attempt to discredit her influence more effectively. Thomas More was executed at the insistence of King Henry VIII for a variety of stated and undeclared reasons, but basically because a dictator of Henry's temperament could not abide even the silent opposition of a man of integrity. In 1600 Giordano Bruno was burnt to death in Rome, ostensibly for adopting theories of astronomy which were deemed to be at variance with the Bible. Yet their author, Copernicus, died peacefully in his bed as a renowned and respected scholar. In our own time Gandhi, Martin Luther King, and Archbishop Oscar Romero have met with similar fates for similar causes. None of them could be accused of direct illegal subversion of the lawful government, yet all of them posed at least an indirect threat to what was unjust in their own societies. In the end it mattered little whether they were killed by the public authorities or by assassins. The deep underlying causes were the threats which they posed to the established order, which had come to terms comfortably with a variety of injustices, such as the English occupation of a large part of France, Henry VIII's succession of wives, or American racial discrimination. Those who profited from such situations had much to fear from the single-minded integrity of the prophets. In an ideal world this class of people would be rewarded as perfect citizens, but in the real world, which supports so much structured and in-built injustice, their deaths were almost inevitable.

In this perspective we should look upon the death of Jesus as the execution of a martyr. It came about ineluctably on account of the vested interests of religious leaders and politicians which were challenged, by implication, by the purity of his religious message with its uncompromising ramifications in the sphere of justice. It was the crowning of his life's work, and his bravery under torture and on the cross has rightly been honoured by Christians and non-Christians ever since.

The respect accorded to the heroic death of a martyr does not explain fully the Christian evaluation of his death. There is more to it than the supreme act of witness to the truth of a cause. Its relationship to the process of the atonement places it in another category altogether, and this delicate problem will be examined in the next chapter.

NOTES

1 So much has been written on this subject that it is difficult to know where to stop. A vast amount of material has been gathered together in a bibliographical article by Werner Georg Kummel, 'Jesus-Forschung seit 1965', *Theologische Rundschau* (Münster, 1980), pp. 293–337. I wish to

draw attention to four books of immediate relevance: H. Küng, *On Being a Christian* (London, 1977), pp. 332ff.; E. Schillebeeckx, *Jesus* (London, 1974), pp. 279ff.; A. Friero, *The Militant Gospel* (London, 1977), pp. 153–5; M. Hengel, *The Cross of the Son of God* (London, 1986), pp. 93–182.

2 The point has been emphasized by Leonardo Boff, *Passion of Christ, Passion of the Whole World* (New York, 1988), p. 14, and *Jesus Christ Liberator* (London, 1978), pp. 105–17.

3 G. Gutiérrez, *The God of Life* (London, 1991), p. 71.

4 Mark 8:31; 9:31; 10:34; and the parallel passages in the other synoptics.

5 Acts 5:36–38; Josephus, *Wars of the Jews*, Book II, 13, 5 and 17, 8.

6 B. Chilton, *The Temple of Jesus: His Sacrificial Program Within a Cultural History of Sacrifice* (Pennsylvania, 1992), especially p. 101.

7 Cf. Friero, op. cit., pp. 153–5.

8 J. L. Segundo, *The Historical Jesus of the Synoptics* (London, 1985), p. 182.

9 The question is discussed in Boff, *Passion of Christ*, op. cit., p. 39; and also by O. Cullmann, *The State in the New Testament* (London, 1975), p. 49, and G. Gutiérrez, *Theology of Liberation* (New York, 1975), pp. 227–30.

10 Küng, op. cit., p. 332.

8

⊠ *Sacrament of the intercession*

Having argued that Christ's work of liberation consists formally in the process of intercession with God the Father, and having presented his death as martyrdom at the hands of his enemies rather than satisfaction required by the Father, I still have two important questions to answer. In what sense can the crucifixion be spoken of as a sacrifice, and what role did it play in the process of the redemption?

I will take the question of sacrifice first, and apply to its elucidation the methodological tool familiar to theologians, namely the concept of analogy. This means that one can see in the crucifixion the essential elements of sacrifice in the usual sense of the term together with sufficient differences to place it in a class of its own. The term 'sacrifice' can be applied to the crucifixion by analogy; and this is the case with many concepts drawn from human experience and applied to God in theology.

My starting point will be the analysis of the elements of sacrifice as presented by R. de Vaux, which were discussed in Chapter 2. Many anthropologists and students of comparative religion have produced descriptions and definitions of sacrifice which are slightly different from that elaborated by de Vaux.[1] However, I prefer to make use of de Vaux's analysis because it represents the understanding of the phenomenon in the minds of Jesus' Jewish contemporaries. It is almost impossible to determine how much the New Testament writers knew about the sacrificial practices of their pagan neighbours, and the religious ideas which accompanied the rituals. It is certain that their own convictions on the matter were formed by the sacrificial liturgies of the Temple in Jerusalem and the instructions about them in the Old Testament. Any attempt to situate the death of Jesus in the context of sacrifice must employ the biblical understanding of sacrifice.

The constituent elements which de Vaux identified were the giving of a gift to God by the worshipper, as a sign of loyalty (and all that goes with this commitment to God); its destruction signified irrevocability; and the performance of the rite in a holy place was to symbolize its transference to the invisible world. If the victim was eaten in part, it was a sign of unity, or rather community with God, and the element of compensation for sin might be present, depending on the circumstances.[2] The reader will see at a glance that the essentials of this understanding of sacrifice were present in the crucifixion in a manner so different from the ordinary Jewish offerings as to place it in a class of its own but without making it so different as to take it out of the category of sacrifice.

The gift to God was the giving up of his life into the hands of his betrayers and executioners. As with the executions of martyrs, this death, which could have been evaded, was the supreme sign of his loyalty and devotion to the Father. This devotion had been expressed in fidelity to his mission which brought upon him the hostility of powerful opponents. Destruction was not symbolic but real, and taken in conjunction with the resurrection it did indeed transfer him to the invisible world with equal reality. Communion with the Father was achieved in a manner vastly superior to the practice of eating part of the victim. The element of atoning for sin was present too, in a way which I will describe further on in this chapter. Thus by using the method of analogy one can see that the crucifixion of Jesus can be spoken of as an authentic sacrifice, without lapsing into merely metaphorical or symbolic language.

The second and more difficult question concerns the role of the crucifixion in the whole causal process of the atonement. Throughout this book I have argued that the reconciliation between the human race and God was effected by the intercession of Jesus, literally asking for our forgiveness. This being so, it is difficult to ascribe a satisfactory role in the process to the crucifixion. Yet this must be attempted in order to do justice to the prominent part which it is accorded by the writers of the New Testament.

In seeking for a solution to this problem I will make use of Karl Rahner's work on the sacraments.[3] He has pioneered a highly original account of the functioning of the sacraments with which to counterbalance a distorted picture inherited from the past.

The Council of Trent, in reaction to Protestantism, had embraced the notion of the quasi-autonomy of the sacraments which had been epitomized in the term *ex opere operato* ('by the performance of the operation'). This expression had never been intended to signify something automatic; it had been elaborated centuries earlier to denote that the sacraments achieved their effects independently of the minister's virtue, or lack of it. It is traceable back to the epoch of persecution in the Roman empire, when Christians cast doubt on the value of sacraments administered by repentant priests and bishops who had compromised their faith in some way under pressure during the period of active persecution. With the passage of time those historical circumstances had been forgotten and in many books and much of the preaching, prior to Vatican II, many Catholics spoke of the sacraments as if they were autonomous. They were also presented in a way which tended to separate them from the Church, and their relationship to grace itself was, to say the least, quantitative. It may be something of an exaggeration, but one could easily have gained the impression from some Catholic writers that grace was a sort of holy fluid which was dispensed from seven bottles to be applied to seven conditions of the soul, such as forgiveness, or matrimony for example.

As a corrective to these popular distortions Karl Rahner suggested that the sacraments must not be treated as if they were the only channels of grace, nor must they be divorced from God's overall salvific work in the world. He stressed that they were above all the visible means of grace, and should be regarded as operations of special intensity, rather like the concentration of light at the focal point of a magnifying glass, so as to produce not just light, but fire.

Rahner's own words on the matter are as follows:

If however the means of grace, its presence, has sacramental structure, that is, based on the unity of grace and its historically manifest concrete embodiment, this must also be true of access to this means or fountain of grace, of entry into it, and of any further acceptance of grace by individuals from it. That does not imply that any and every conferring and acceptance of the grace present in the Church as the fundamental sacrament, has in every case the nature of a sacrament in the strictest and technical sense of the word. It has been sufficiently indicated already, and we cannot go into the matter further here, that any grace-giving event has a quasi-sacramental structure and shares in Christ's character as both divine and human. But when the Church in her official, organized, public capacity precisely as the source of redemptive grace meets the individual in the actual ultimate accomplishment of her nature, there we have the sacraments in the proper sense, and they can be seen to be the essential functions that bring into activity the very essence of the Church herself. For in them she herself attains the highest degree of actualization of what she always is: the presence of redemptive grace for men, historically visible and manifest as the sign of the eschatologically victorious grace of God in the world.[4]

To that account of the working of the sacraments I would like to add a complementary notion, drawn from the Old Testament. We should look upon them as channels of covenanted grace. This means that we can count upon the achievement of their effects with a sense of security, because they have been promised by God, although we cannot thereby place a strict claim upon him, which would be incompatible with the gratuity of grace. In this way the believer can receive the sacraments with confidence, yet not treat them as automatic producers of grace.

Thanks to Rahner and others the concept of sacrament has been widened beyond the classical seven, and is used in other cases where the bestowal of grace takes place with particular intensity, and at the same time is made visible in a symbolic way. In this sense the term has been applied to the Church itself, and this usage was sanctioned by the Second Vatican Council in its decree on the Church, *Lumen Gentium*:

By her relationship with Christ, the Church is a kind of sacrament, or sign of intimate union with God, and of the unity of all mankind. She is also an instrument for the achievement of such union and unity.[5]

The use of the term 'sacrament' for the Church as a whole indicates that it is the visible manifestation of God's saving action in the world. In this way it underlines the all-important point that the activities of God's grace among the human race are not to be limited to the conscious transactions among the believing members of the visible Church. It leaves open the whole vast field of operations by which the grace of God comes to individuals outside the ranks of the Church, which I discussed earlier in the book in the context of the salvation of the unevangelized peoples. It has provided a healthy corrective to the erstwhile attitude that everything concerning the liberation of the human race from sin was taking place inside the structures of the visible Church.

I wish to apply these ideas on sacramentality to the crucifixion. Basically the death on the cross marks the point of greatest intensity in Jesus' atoning mission. It was here that his task of leading the human race back to reconciliation with the Father reached its apogee and maximum intensity. At the risk of seeming to present a mere truism, one must insist that it was visible, and as such it served as a symbol for the whole process. In this heroic acceptance of a violent death he provided us with a visible manifestation for the other aspects of the sequence of events which are not open to human inspection, namely the resurrection and the intercession in eternity which is spoken of most clearly in the Letter to the Hebrews. The fact of visible manifestation is important. Although the risen Christ was seen by his disciples after his being raised from the dead, the resurrection itself was not witnessed by any human being. That is why it has featured less frequently in Christian art in comparison with the crucifixion, and possibly too why its role in the whole redemptive process has been overlooked until quite recently. It is obvious too that the act of intercession at the right hand of the Father is not visible to human perception. All aspects of the work of atonement find their maximum actualization and visible symbolic manifestation in the crucifixion. For that reason I feel that one is entitled to speak of the crucifixion as the sacrament of Christ's intercession.

Rahner himself came close to this notion in one of his books. He spoke of the crucifixion as a sign. To quote his own words:

The cross is the *signum efficax*, the efficacious sign, of the redeeming love that communicates God himself, because the cross establishes God's love in the world in a definitive and historically irreversible way . . . Given these presuppositions the cross of Christ can really be seen as the efficacious sign of God's salvific will in the world.[6]

Rahner repudiates the notion of an angry God requiring vengeance, but he does not develop further the precise process of the causality in the whole economy of redemption.

An example drawn from another area of life may help to illustrate the matter by way of comparison. One can apply the foregoing ideas to marriage. When two people exchange their consent in the presence of the priest and other witnesses, they conclude a relationship which is thenceforward public and will be recognized by society. The brief ritual symbolizes a relationship which did not start then, and certainly will continue long after that ceremony has ended. It also makes a pronouncement about the physical manifestation of their love whose intimacies are naturally secluded from public intrusion. Quite apart from a church wedding, the ceremony in a town hall or register office also has a quasi-sacramental character insofar as it encapsulates a point of intense deliberateness in the enunciation of this relationship and makes it manifest to the world at large.

With these considerations in mind I consider that it is legitimate to speak of the crucifixion as the sacrament of Christ's intercession. This safeguards the causal roles of all the other factors which entered into the liberating process, and co-ordinates their mutual interrelation. It does justice to what the New Testament teaches about the death on the cross, as well as the resurrection and role of Christ's intercession in the work of the atonement.

The theory which I have proposed does not deny the causal role of the crucifixion of Jesus, but shifts the centre of gravity to his intercession, which I maintain is the principal cause of the atonement. By expressing it thus I hope to restore a measure of balance to the matter which had been distorted since the time of St Anselm. In the New Testament and the Fathers the crucifixion is never put forward as if it were the sole cause of our reconciliation with God. The resurrection was accorded its rightful place in the process in the pages of the Scriptures, and some of the Greek Fathers spoke as if they considered the incarnation itself to be the sufficient cause of the atonement.

The Church's magisterium has made no pronouncement on the matter which could settle the identification of the precise cause. After St Anselm had put forward his theory of satisfaction a gradual distortion of the theology took place. The crucifixion was presented as the all-sufficient compensation for sin, and all other elements in the work of atonement were ignored in practice.

It is my contention that this distortion can be remedied by focusing on the other elements of Christ's work, and devising a way of relating them to the crucifixion. The principal outcome of this reappraisal is to recognize that the main cause in the reconciliation of the human race to God was Christ's asking for forgiveness on our behalf, in other words intercession. The crucifixion is the quasi-sacramental manifestation of the whole process and its point of most intense operation in the world of time. Thus it has become the epitome of the total work of redemption, and the focus of theology, religious art, and popular piety.

NOTES

1 For example E. O. James, *The Origins of Sacrifice* (London, 1933), pp. 256, 257; R. K. Yerkes, *Sacrifice in Greek and Roman Religions and Early Judaism* (London, 1953), passim.
2 R. de Vaux, *Ancient Israel, Its Life and Institutions* (London, 1961), pp. 451–4.
3 K. Rahner, *The Church and the Sacraments* (London, 1963).
4 Rahner, op. cit., p. 22.
5 *Lumen Gentium*, sections 1 and 9. The same usage can be read in the document on the Liturgy, *Sacrosanctum Concilium*, section 26; English translations in W. A. Abbott (ed.), *The Documents of Vatican II* (New York/London, 1966), pp. 15, 16, 147.
6 K. Rahner, *Theological Investigations*, vol. 21 (London, 1988), p. 250.